In this unique manual, three top German trainers have joined forces to share their considerable knowledge and experience of producing superbly trained horses and riders, from novice to Grand Prix.

The late **Dr Wolfgang Hölzel** grew up at his parents' riding school so his riding career began at an early age. He was so outstanding in dressage, show jumping and eventing that he received the coveted Gold Medal for riders (Reiterabzeichen). For nine years he was head of training at the famous German Riding School at Warendorf, and afterwards became national trainer for the Australian dressage and three-day event teams, a post he held for six years.

Dr Petra Hölzel, a doctor of philology and a passionate rider from childhood, trained horses with her husband, up to advanced level. Together they published many books and articles on the subject.

Martin Plewa, author of the chapter on jumping, has been riding since the age of six. He has been trained in all disciplines up to advanced level. As an event rider he has competed in world and European championships. He is the author of many articles in specialist books and magazines. He has been the national trainer of the German three-day event team since 1985.

DRESSAGE TIPS
AND
Training Solutions

Using the German Training System

Dressage Tips by PETRA and WOLFGANG HÖLZEL
Jumping Tips by MARTIN PLEWA

Translated by Claudia Staubitz

Trafalgar Square Publishing

First published in the United States of America in 1995 by
Trafalgar Square Publishing
North Pomfret
Vermont 05053

First published in paperback 2001

English language edition published simultaneously in the United States
of America by Trafalgar Square Publishing and Great Britain by
Kenilworth Press Ltd

© 1995, Kenilworth Press Ltd

First published in Germany under the title *Profitips für Reiter,* by
Franckh-Kosmos Verlags GmbH & Co., Stuttgart, in 1992.

© 1992, Franckh-Kosmos Verlags-GmbH & Co., Stuttgart

Produced by Kenilworth Press Ltd, Addington,
Buckingham, MK18 2JR, England

Printed and bound in Great Britain

ISBN 1-57076-207-4

Disclaimer of Liability
The Authors and Publisher shall have neither liability nor
responsibility to any person or entity with respect to any loss or
damage caused or alleged to be caused directly or indirectly by the
information contained in this book. While the book is as accurate as the
authors can make it, there may be errors, omissions, and inaccuracies.

Text design by Paul Saunders

For Manne

CONTENTS

PREFACE

This is essentially a training manual for those occasions when things do not work out the way they are described in most other books on dressage. It offers concise instruction in classical dressage for horses and riders, from novice to advanced, using the German training system, which we have taught at national level for many years. It is not a book for complete beginners, but assumes a certain level of accomplishment on the part of the reader.

Rather than an ongoing narrative, the training advice is arranged as a series of tips concerning particular movements and exercises, with questions and answers identifying problems and offering solutions to overcome them.

This book is not intended to be read from cover to cover; rather, it can be dipped into at leisure or whenever the need arises. You can browse through the various training sections, or go straight to the page which concerns a problem you are grappling with right now. For example: if flying changes are a problem and your horse is changing late behind, you will find sound advice on how to correct this fault. And if you read the hints on the basic training needed in connection with your problem, then you may also discover what aspect of your horse's schooling

Wolfgang Hölzel

has been neglected in the first place and so put matters right.

We are particularly keen that readers should study the sections on sympathetic management of the horse and training the rider's mind, in Chapter 1. Many problems in the training of horses would not occur at all if their physical and psychological requirements were recognised and taken into consideration. In appreciating these needs you provide the first and most decisive condition for success in the horse's training.

We believe that rider psychology and the way the rider trains himself to think, are vitally important in the schooling of horses. This approach has proved to be very effective in many other sports, and it can be applied with equal success to dressage. Whether you are an instructor or pupil, if you are having problems in developing your own skills as a rider or in schooling your horse, you will find a host of ideas to help overcome these difficulties.

Perhaps surprisingly in a book about dressage, we have also included a chapter on jumping, with numerous gymnastic exercises to complement the horse's flatwork training.

We hope that in reading this book you will gain many useful insights into training horses, and that you will be able to use them to develop your own skills as a rider and to enhance the performance of your horse.

Dr Petra Hölzel
Dr Wolfgang Hölzel
Martin Plewa

TRANSLATOR'S NOTE

There are three essential principles of dressage training which in German are expressed quite simply in a single word, but which unfortunately have no direct equivalents in the English language. They are: *Losgelassenheit, Durchlässigkeit* and *Schwung*. In English they are roughly, and rather inadequately, translated as looseness, submission, and swing (or 'swinging through the back', or even just 'impulsion'). In the interests of keeping the text flowing and uncomplicated, these basic translations have been adopted in this book, but for the reader to reap the full benefits of the 'tips' it is important to understand the wider implications of these terms. Here, then, are three short definitions which should be read into the text each time you come across the German terms.

Losgelassenheit (looseness)

Translated literally this means 'letting loose(ness)' and implies a state of relaxation, both mentally and physically. To achieve this, muscles and joints are to be used in a natural,

unrestrained manner, with maximum efficiency and minimum strain, while the horse's attitude should be one of calmness and concentration. In this state he can use his energy to its full extent because he is not tense, afraid or tired and therefore shows no resistance. The outward signs can clearly be observed in a 'losgelassen' horse – he goes forward rhythmically and energetically, with loose muscles and a swinging back; he carries his tail; and his ears and facial expression signal his concentration on the rider's aids. It is self-evident that the rider needs the same level of Losgelassenheit in order to sit quietly and smoothly and give soft, sensitive and effective aids.

Durchlässigkeit (submission)

Of the three technical expressions discussed here, this one suffers the most distortion when translated into English. To equate it to 'submission' puts too much emphasis on complete obedience and overlooks the way of going. Again, the literal translation shows where the German term is pointing – 'a state of letting through'. This 'letting-through' embraces the aids, the energy, the movement, and eventually, when it has developed, the Schwung. Regarding the aids, this does not only mean that the horse lets the rein aids through to the hindquarters, but also, and much more importantly, that he lets the driving aids through from the hindquarters back into the rider's hands. Further, there has to be a willing reaction to lateral and weight aids. It is obvious that such willing and prompt reaction to the aids can only be provided by a 'losgelassen' horse, who has no mental or physical tension or resistance in the way he co-operates with a sensitive and knowledgeable rider.

Schwung (swing)

Sometimes people are described as having a certain 'spring in their step', and the same combination of physical and mental implications is contained in the German expression 'Schwung'. In general it describes a containment and redirection of energy that allows forward movement which comes from the whole body lifting itself out of the restraints of gravity for a split-second with each step. A well-trained dressage horse gains increasingly more forward impulsion from his hindquarters, and this, together with a well-developed topline, allows him to swing through his back and therefore move his limbs freely and efficiently, almost like a puppet on a string. His athletic power, Losgelassenheit and subsequently 'durchlässig' attitude allow him to submit all his energy and ability to the demands of the task the rider is setting, gaining ground with elastic, bouncy steps and eventually giving expression to his energy in the grace and suspension of a passage or the concentrated power of a canter pirouette.

Claudia Staubitz
May 1995

ACKNOWLEDGEMENTS

The authors would like to thank C. Hess and S. Hopmann of the German National Equestrian Federation for their expert advice, which has contributed valuable information to our tips.

PICTURE CREDITS

Photographs
BMfLufWein – 150
Czerny – 16, 59, 61, 77, 82
Ernst – 53, 88, 89, 90, 110, 130, 131, 142, 145, 147
Hölzel – 7, 14, 15, 18, 21, 31, 40, 41, 46, 50, 51, 86, 93, 100, 104, 113, 116, 118, 121, 123, 126, 149, 151, 155, 156 (top)
Parry – 156 (bottom)
Plewa – 70

Line drawings
The line illustrations are by Gisela Holstein.

1

TRAINING CONSIDERED

1.1 SYMPATHETIC MANAGEMENT OF THE HORSE

Your horse should be cared for and managed in a way that reflects his natural needs. In this way you cater for his physical and mental health, which is essential if you are to achieve success in his training.

Your horse is first and foremost an animal whose natural instinct is to be constantly moving, and he needs exercise just as much as he needs food and water – a horse in the wild is on the move for up to sixteen hours a day. This means that his muscles are constantly exercised, his joints are kept supple, his respiratory organs are supplied with fresh air, blood circulates through his heart and lungs, and daylight stimulates his metabolism.

You may contend that the modern riding horse is very different from a wild horse because it has become thoroughly domesticated over thousands of years of breeding. This is true, but his basic needs have remained more or less the same.

The horse's need for exercise is nowhere near satisfied by an hour's work a day. You can certainly work your horse hard in this hour, but he will still suffer if he is confined to his loose-box for the other twenty-three hours. The same applies to the rest day customarily observed in many yards: try to avoid it where possible.

Always remember that insufficient exercise can lead to many health problems: weakness of the tendons, ligaments and joints, and diseases of the respiratory system are some of the unfortunate consequences.

Moreover, your horse is very much a herd animal and only feels comfortable and safe in the company of other horses: if you ignore his social needs, behavioural problems may occur. Thus social contact between horses – that is, the chance to make eye contact and sniff at each other – should be made possible by stabling in open loose-boxes.

More exercise is necessary

In his normal one hour of work a day, the domesticated horse misses out on the opportunity for lengthy periods of quiet, slow exercise that the wild horse enjoys. The stabled horse therefore needs *additional forms of exercise* in order to satisfy his physical requirements to the full, ones which will use his store of energy in a natural way. This means exercise that makes him healthier and happier, because without having to concentrate on a rider there is no demand on his nerves or his mental state.

Therefore, make sure he gets plenty of unregimented exercise, like strolling through the countryside, or being turned out, or led out for a walk on a lead rein. This is important if he is to keep a steady equilibrium both mentally and physically and if his performance is not to suffer.

Perhaps you think you don't have time for these activities? Well, if not, you owe it to your horse to think of something, and there is a range of possibilities each of which involves hardly any extra time:

• Turn out for several hours of exercise in a field or paddock (tips on how to avoid the inherent risks are given below). A clipped horse wearing a New Zealand rug can go out in most weathers.

• Lunge in a headcollar (halter – US). The time saved in tacking up and attaching side-reins can be used for longer exercise.

• Ask a groom to ride the horse at walk for an hour a day (in addition to schooling work). In a school or arena, this can even be done when a lesson is going on.

The horse's natural instinct is to be constantly moving, and he therefore needs more exercise than just an hour's schooling a day. Turning him out is the most natural way for him to take additional exercise.

Long periods of quiet grazing are essential for your horse's physical and mental health.

• Your instructor could ride or lead your horse at walk while teaching.

• Ride one horse and lead another. This can be done with or without side-reins. It is best if two horses can be taken out hacking, but they could also be exercised in an arena.

• Turn out in an indoor arena. If the horse is used to it, he can be left without supervision, but to avoid injuries every horse should first be lunged or walked for ten minutes.

• Some professional riders have found it a useful practice to turn out a number of horses that know each other well, loose in an indoor arena, then to pick out one at a time and work it.

• Exercise in a horse-walker. This not ideal, but is certainly better than no exercise at all.

So you see, there are plenty of possibilities. Sometimes it is simply a matter of overcoming long-established, lazy habits. Always bear in mind that it is better to ride or lunge without a saddle if time is short, and to use the time saved for extra exercise. For riding at walk you don't necessarily have to change into jodhpurs and full riding gear – you can do this in your jeans!

More exercise solves problems

Additional quiet exercise is also an important way of improving your horse's alertness and outlook on life. In a wild horse the sensory organs have to process a multitude of stimuli generated by his surroundings and assess them correctly as harmless or dangerous.

Stable vices such as weaving, crib-biting or windsucking are the outcome of insufficient exercise, variety and

social contact, all of which result in boredom. High spirits and disobedience – often the cause of riding accidents – are usually generated because a long day spent in the stable is so completely lacking in stimulus. The horse therefore becomes unnaturally susceptible to the impact of his environment when he leaves the monotony of his stable routine.

Remember: Additional exercise is an excellent means of alleviating many of the problems which occur when the horse is ridden. Your horse might be quite transformed by it.

Field or paddock

Turning your horse out – if at all possible with another friendly horse – is the most beneficial and natural form of exercise for him. If no paddock is available the horse owner should do everything in his power and within his

financial means to give his horse the exercise that is so vital to his species.

It is *important to prepare the horse carefully for turning out and particularly in the company of other horses.* Understandably, many owners, especially those with valuable competition horses, are worried about the risk of injury to horses which are not accustomed to being turned out. There are some rules that should be followed:

• Only turn your horse out after it has been worked.

• Don't feed beforehand, then his appetite for grass will keep him entirely occupied and prevent him from wildly careering about.

• Stay with him for a while, watch him, and if necessary, try to calm him.

• It has also been proved useful to take a new horse into the paddock on the lunge. You can then control and channel his high spirits until he becomes used to his new freedom and starts grazing quietly.

By nature the horse is a herd animal and this basic characteristic is answered most appropriately by turning him out with one or a number of other horses, but you must be particularly careful when you put two horses together for the first time. Observe their reactions closely. After the initial curious sniffing either a fight or a peaceful companionship will ensue. If the latter, you can leave them to themselves, but if they start to kick and bite you will have to separate them immediately; on no account put the two rivals back into a field together, especially if they have shoes on, as they could injure each other quite badly.

Before two horses are turned out together for the first time, it is a good idea to ask the farrier to remove their shoes. Without shoes they cannot hurt each other seriously and you can wait to see if they get on. Afterwards they can be shod again.

An older, quiet horse which is used to being turned out, may well be a suitable companion for a newcomer, and such a pair will often become inseparable. This is fine; your new horse and his quiet companion will graze happily for long periods. A horse on his own, however, soon becomes agitated, paces up and down in front of the gate and may become so worked up that he sweats heavily.

So unless your horse is a loner, which is very rare, do provide him with a companion. Be aware, however, that problems can arise with bigger groups, where a newcomer is often treated as an intruder because he disturbs the established hierarchy of the herd. This can lead to fights, although things do not necessarily become serious because horses understand and react to threats very promptly. If the new horse does not find a partner he may start to graze quietly at a respectful distance from the others. Up to this point you should simply observe events and only

Unconstrained exercise on a leisurely walk.

A horse is most content when turned out with a companion.

interfere in an emergency.

A good and safe alternative are individual paddocks where horses can make contact over the fence. When they become accustomed to each other and show no signs of animosity they can usually be turned out together without problems, though you should still keep an eye on the group for a while.

Stable management

If you are able to keep your horse in a loose-box in a large open barn together with other horses, then you have found the ideal way of keeping a horse stabled. Unfortunately this is not practical or possible for everyone, but even if you keep your horse on his own in a separate loose-box you can still do a great deal to fulfil his needs. Make

sure his box is as large and light as possible. An opening to the outside can easily be installed so that your horse has enough air and light, and can thereby make contact with the outside world and with horses in neighbouring stables.

Straight stalls are quite unacceptable, and no horse should ever be kept under such conditions.

You can partially satisfy the social needs of your horse by spending as much time with him as possible. This is best spent engaged in non-stressful outdoor exercise, such as going for leisurely rides or walking him out on the lead-rein in the countryside; you could even take him for a paddle in a lake or stream.

• *Note:* If you can satisfy your horse's natural requirements you will minimise or avoid altogether many of the problems that can arise in his training.

1.2 PRINCIPLES OF TRAINING

• The following order of objectives should be observed when planning your horse's long-term training as well as in each successive stage:

1. Looseness (Losgelassenheit) and suppleness on both reins (bend).

2. Steady contact and submissiveness (Durchlässigkeit), where the horse is in balance, but without elevation in his movement. (The points described under 1 and 2 are identified as 'basic schooling work'.)

3. Collection, with the corresponding elevation and simultaneous development of impulsion (Schwung).

4. Relaxation.

With an advanced, well-ridden horse these different stages pass into each other in a relatively short time, but their sequence should be strictly adhered to.

• With young and problem horses the basic schooling work as set out in points 1 and 2 (looseness/Losgelassenheit and submissiveness/Durchlässigkeit) is the purpose of the whole first stage of training. It is the foundation and cornerstone of all further training, not only for dressage but also for show jumping and eventing.

When a horse is turned out for the first time it is advisable to stay close at hand for a while and if necessary, calm him down.

IMPORTANT In every stage of training it is most important to ride for ten minutes at walk before and after each session. A horse brought straight out of his loose-box must be given the chance to warm up and lubricate his joints, which is necessary for their flexibility.

In cold weather it is sensible to ride the horse in a rug for the first ten minutes (especially if he is clipped). And by riding in walk at the end of the session you ensure that he is breathing normally and taken back to his box in a physically and mentally relaxed condition.

• Only after the basic schooling work has been successfully consolidated can we think about collection, and even then it is introduced carefully and very gradually. Looseness (Losgelassenheit) must be a priority throughout the exercises teaching collection, and horse should always be ready to stretch at any stage, even when he is working at the highest degree of collection. Submission (Durchlässigkeit) is also consolidated and refined throughout this work.

Two strange horses sniff each other in the paddock...

...either a fight will follow...

...or the two will start grazing together peacefully.

3. Extreme collection; required to perform up to Grand Prix level (full canter pirouette, piaffe, passage).

• Take care to develop the horse's impulsion (Schwung) (by lengthening the strides in trot and canter) at the same rate as you work to collect him. Even in the same session it is a good idea to alternate between work which to develops the driving power, and exercises which increase the carrying power of the hindquarters.

• Set yourself a goal for each training session and plan its structure accordingly. Stress certain points: improve on exercises that the horse has already learnt, and/or introduce a new lesson; however, do not expect him to perform his whole repertoire in each session.

There are three stages of collection:

1. Elementary collection; the beginnings of collection are expected in Novice and Elementary tests.

2. Medium collection; this is required in Medium tests and the easier Advanced tests.

• Quite apart from his daily schooling, the horse as a naturally mobile animal needs additional exercise (see above). You will be able to assess how much he requires when you come to control his forwardness – tension and surplus energy will make him too strong.

• Try to provide variety in the course of a week's work – for example, you could lunge him, school him over trotting poles, hack him out, do some gymnastic jumping, loose school him, walk him out on a lead-rein, turn him out, each of which is a clearly different form of exercise from concentrated school work.

• Take care to make every single training session interesting, and use all three paces. If the focal point of one day's exercises lies in trot, then use the canter more when you loosen the horse up and to relax him at the end, and vice versa. Work on dressage movements during a hack, or use the arena just to loosen the horse up and to ask for a basic degree of submission (Durchlässigkeit).

• Many riders ride for too long on one rein, or clearly prefer one rein. Try to get into the habit of changing the rein every 4-5 minutes (use your watch!); out hacking this means changing the trot diagonal or canter lead regularly.

Remember: A period of relaxation should not only be included after a whole session, it is also important and gymnastically effective after any exercise that is new or especially taxing. Similarly, a period at walk is a good idea after each part of a training session; for the horse this constitutes a rest and a reward.

Open-fronted loose-boxes offer the opportunity for social contact, which horses need.

• It is best to teach something new at the end of a session, so that after the first roughly successful try you can finish, praise your horse, let him walk and give him a long rein. Do not ride the exercise again on the same day.

• Always start with the easiest form of any new exercise, before you ask for greater precision – practise it in approximate form before attempting to ride it accurately. For instance, ride the piaffe with a clear forward tendency first of all and only gradually ride it more and more on the spot. Give rhythm priority over expression.

• Take advantage of the horse's excellent memory: he will clearly remember your praise when he performs an exercise successfully and will try hard to do it as well the next time.

• 'Tune' the horse constantly to your aids, which should be as light and unobtrusive as possible. Insist on an immediate response to every aid.

• Become accustomed to riding to the clock. This is the only way to keep a check on the time you spend working at different parts of a session, on the intervals of relaxation in between and the whole session.

Take care: Check yourself, too, as often as you can: mirrors, videos and the judgement of competent observers are an important guide.

• Avoid overtaxing your horse and never forget that pleasure and enjoyment provide the motivation for the highest achievements, and put horse and rider at ease in their work together.

• Consider your horse's health: arrange for the vet to vaccinate him regularly and to check his teeth, and worm him at regular intervals. A blood test will reveal nutritional deficiencies and the presence of parasites in the blood. Provide plenty of air, light and exercise to keep your horse's physical functions in order, and avoid dust in any shape or form. The type and amount of feed needs to be controlled and regulated; usually too much is given in relation to the amount of exercise the horse receives. Make it a rule to check his legs, hoofs and back, especially where the saddle lies.

Remember: Only a healthy horse can be a contented and capable partner.

1.3 TRAINING THE RIDER'S MIND

Note: The contents of this section and many exercises in it, stem from conversations with and lectures by Dr Eberspächer, Professor of Sports Psychology, Heidelberg University.

In the following section we discuss a way to approach learning and training which controls and improves physical performance through the rider's ability to concentrate his own mind. With the help of this approach great success has been achieved in almost all disciplines. However, it can only be effective if you try it out and practise it in the long term. That is the same with any form of training: if you only start trying it out a short time before an examination or competition it will produce little result.

However, used consistently, for a competition and throughout the preparation for it, the rider's ability to concentrate his mind can be of great advantage. The ability to visualise movements means you can run through them on your 'inner film-screen' as often as you want to, without putting unnecessary strain on your horse. By carefully directing and training your concentration you can succeed in shutting out distractions and thus channel all your energy and ability towards the task in hand.

Finally, a positive attitude will help you to keep your composure even if you make mistakes, and also to control nervousness, because you will be confident of being able to do certain things, and of being able to do them under any circumstances, in any arena in the world.

This approach to training is not only a key to success, it also enables you to enjoy your sport more. By developing your awareness of your own body you will be able to sense the horse's movement more consciously and intensely; you will learn to 'listen in', to 'feel your way' with heightened sensitivity and will increasingly fine-tune your aids. And in learning to control and improve your feel and your influence on the horse through your mind, you will be able to recognise and appreciate the progress you make quite independently from the prizes won in competition.

Spheres of application

There are five important spheres where this approach to training can be of use:

1. *Relaxation* You learn how to relax systematically and under any circumstances and thereby create the optimal conditions for your body to function. Being able to do this will serve you especially well if you find yourself in a difficult or strange situation and also under stressful and test conditions.

2. *Body-feel* You learn to sense every part of your body consciously and thus to control it better.

3. *Conception of movement* You learn to think through a movement and the way it develops as precisely and vividly as if it were real. This can evolve to such an extreme that your body reacts in tune with your imagination and you consequently perform a movement just by thinking through it.

4. *Concentration* You learn to concentrate absolutely in every situation, and do not allow yourself to be distracted by disturbances. You might practise this by aiming to exclude environmental factors or personal anger for the period of a set task. You also train yourself to get over mistakes, so that you are able to concentrate immediately and exclusively on the next exercise.

5. *Positive outlook and self-confidence* You learn to think positively and to develop a healthy self-confidence. Develop an awareness of what you are capable of – and be a little proud of it. This will help you to believe yourself capable of the things you cannot (yet) do. The goals you set yourself have to be realistic, though, and in relation to what is possible under your

circumstances; this means you must be sensible and self-critical. Always formulate what you want to achieve in a positive way: thus don't keep telling yourself what you must not do, but what you should do – not what is wrong, but how to do it right.

Practical exercises and examples

1. Relaxation

In order to perform at your best in exceptional situations such as examinations and tests, you need to feel a certain tension and excitement, as this leads to that well-known rush of adrenalin in the blood. However, if the tension becomes too acute, stress – with its typical symptoms of sweating, and accelerated, flat breathing and heart-beat – takes over. This can lead to under-achievement, and reactions which are slower or even wrong. For this sort of situation you need an effective relaxation exercise that you can rely on.

The following shoulder-breathing exercise has proved to be an excellent aid to relaxation, helpful and effective even in situations which impose the greatest stress such as a World Championship or an Olympic Games. However, it can only be successful if it is practised over a long period of time, well in advance of any particular competition.

Go through every single step and try it out:

• Pull both shoulders up in the direction of your ears, and even higher.

• Let them slowly sink back down.

• Now pull your shoulders back right up to your ears, breathe in deeply at the same time, and hold your breath and your shoulders for six or seven seconds.

• Count: 21, 22, 23, 24, 25, 26 – then breathe out slowly and let your shoulders sink back down at the same time.

After just a few times of performing this exercise you will notice that your muscles relax and you feel better. Nor does it take much time to do, and you can practise it almost anywhere, sitting down or standing up. In time you will be able to utilise its tension-reducing and relaxing effect in stress-inducing situations such as examinations or competitions.

On a horse you should practise the exercise at first in halt, then later at the walk. As soon as you find that you can successfully reduce tension even in stressful situations, then you can begin to shorten the exercise. At the first sign of tension make a conscious effort to breathe out deeply; soon you will realise that this alone can produce a pleasant sensation of relaxation.

In its shortened form you can effectively apply the exercise at any time, in a competition, even when you are actually riding a dressage test or jumping course, or in theoretical examinations.

2. Body-feel

A pronounced and precise awareness of your own body is especially important for equestrian disciplines, because it is only once you have achieved a high degree of sensitivity that you can influence, and therefore improve, your horse's paces and posture, and the exercises that you do, and your own seat and aids.

Your trainer's advice and guidance may have a short-term effect, but you will not make any significant, long-term improvement if you have not learnt to feel, test out, and improve on what he or she is trying to tell you. Developing a sensitive and precise feeling for your own body is by no means easy – but it can be achieved!

> **IMPORTANT** Before you can begin to feel every part of your body it must be free of tension, as tension will block sensitivity, i.e. the body must be in a state of relaxation.

Start by consciously trying to sense an awareness of the different parts of your body – for example, every single finger of your right and then your left hand, or your toes, one after the other. Most people can only do this by moving their toes or fingers and that is perfectly normal! It takes some practice to feel any given limb on demand, without moving it.

Next train your sensory faculties to be aware of larger strands of muscles: the shoulders, the upper and lower arms, the thighs and the calves. Also try to experience how these parts feel in intensive movement.

In this manner, learn to feel your way through the whole of your body, limb by limb, from head to toe. Include the joints too – neck, hip-joint, wrists and ankles. Concentrate particularly on the centre of movement, the hips.

First test all of this when not on the horse, sitting or lying down. Then try it out in the saddle, first in halt, later at

walk as you warm up or during the intervals at walk. At the same time check the essential points of your seat and aids, for instance the position of your calves, the amount of pressure from your leg that is required to drive the horse on, and feel your ring-finger and your hands and the way they relate to the horse's mouth.

Later on, use every opportunity in trot and in canter, and also in every exercise, to refine your awareness of your body, and thereby to control and improve the movement you are performing at the time. The more you are able consciously to experience exactly how a successfully executed exercise should feel, the easier it will be to ride it again in exactly the same way. Success will not be a product of chance any more, but part of your experience, and one which you will be able to summon up at any time.

This is also your trainer's most important responsibility: he should help you to become increasingly sensitive to your own movements, and to those of the horse. From the ground he checks your seat and aids, and the horse's rhythm, impulsion (Schwung), and the activity of the back; he will comment on contact, submission (Durchlässigkeit), and collection, and the way you ride different exercises, and he should be able to convey to you a feeling for their correct execution. By asking the right questions and leading you to the right experiences he should help you to develop your own sense of purpose and control.

3. Conception of movement

Learn to go through movements in your mind very precisely, as if you were really performing them. Your nerves, muscles, tendons and ligaments react more subtly but in the same way as in the real movement; and the fascinating thing is that once you are performing in reality, you will react exactly as you did in your mind!

This means that in your mind you ride every single detail of a jumping course or dressage test, and also express verbally everything you are doing; this demands maximum self-control, and it enables your trainer to scrutinise the way you go about things. You learn to feel well-performed exercises with closed eyes, and to repeat them afterwards in the same way.

A shortened reiteration of the right movements should help you to ride the exercise in exactly the same way, again and again. Train yourself to feel and see in your mind's eye everything you do in practice both beforehand and afterwards, like an 'inner film' with all its specific details, and also introduce certain moments of intense concentration.

Preliminary exercises

• Start by visualising simple, familiar things such as the view of a certain house, or a lake or river.

• Then try to imagine as precisely as possible an event containing many sensual impressions: close your eyes and imagine for instance that you are lying on a beach. You can see the sea in a certain colour; you can feel your relaxed body in the warm sunlight; you can feel the sand underneath you and hear the waves.

• Establish which sensual impression was the strongest. If the optical impression – the colour of the sea – was the most intense, then you will know that for you, visual perception will be most helpful when later you wish to recall something; so for example you will be able to imagine a movement most effectively with the help of the visual impressions associated with it.

Remember: To start with, stop trying to think through a movement as soon as the impressions become weaker: don't try to force yourself to see the image more clearly, because in time this sort of recollection will happen spontaneously and it will stay in your mind for longer and increasingly more clearly. Finish the exercise by breathing deeply and opening your eyes.

Exercises with images of movements

• Begin with simple, shorter images of movements; for example see yourself walking, swimming, galloping, jumping or hacking out.

• In time build up your perception with many more elements of certain movements, such as excerpts from a dressage test, or a series of jumps in a show-jumping or cross-country course. Tell yourself what you are doing.

• Here is an example exercise in which you imagine and feel a transition from trot to walk over four or five strides. Read the paragraph on page 50-51 once. Then close your eyes and imagine the following very positively and feel it very intensely: you are riding in a familiar arena – you can see the arena, the letters and the mirrors, maybe you can even smell a familiar smell (the horse's sweat, perhaps the arena's surface material). You are riding on the left rein in working trot, and you can feel the powerful thrust with which your horse pushes himself along; your calves stay rhythmically and lightly against the horse's sides, and his back is swinging; in your hands, on your ring-finger you can feel the even, elastic contact with the horse's mouth.

Now your calves drive the horse on slightly more actively into your closed, gently restraining hands, while your seat slides elastically forwards. You can feel how your horse carries himself more, his hindquarters coming increasingly beneath him, how he fills the space between your calves and how his movement takes you with him. Now he wants to halt, but you use your calves to keep the trot rhythm going and let your hands become a little lighter. Feel the shorter steps, and now allow the horse to walk, at the same time thinking of driving on in the rhythm of the walk.

In the practical execution of a trot-to-walk transition, you will not be able to 'play' the whole of this detailed film, especially in examinations or competitions. For this reason it is important to reduce it to a short formula that you can use at any time, such as, for example: calves – restraining hand – seat – lighter hand – walk.

• Expand these images of movements to include, say, a whole dressage test or jumping course, and then make your short version of it.

• Commit to your memory certain points that you must pay attention to.

Perhaps you have problems with rhythm and your horse tends to rush in medium trot – so, make the corner beforehand rounder, and start lengthening the strides even before that corner, so that the approach to medium trot becomes longer.

Or: in the halt and salute from canter your horse tends to stop dead and fall onto his forehand – take care to perform half-halts rather earlier, and maybe allow a few trot strides, though make sure that he takes his weight on his hindquarters and stays straight.

> **IMPORTANT** Always tell yourself what you are intending to do, and not what you have to avoid.

4. Concentration

If you want to do well in stressful situations such as examinations or competitions, you must develop the ability to concentrate on the matter in hand for every single second and to shut out any disturbance factors. We are not born with this ability, but we can acquire it.

Exercises

• Begin, as described above, by training your mind to visualise images and events. Don't worry if at first other thoughts interfere, such as the row with your parents or problems at work for instance; this is perfectly normal.

• Do not try to repress those thoughts altogether because they will only keep recurring more strongly; rather put them off until later. In your imagination make a note of them and put them into a 'problem-letterbox', at the same time promising yourself to address that problem later. And keep this promise at all costs!

• Build up your visualising of movements until you are thinking through more complex sequences such as an actual test or jumping course. Practise this when there are other disturbances: the radio playing, when you are wearing headphones, people talking in the same room and so on.

• Resolve to do certain tests at certain times with your horse, and simulate the real thing even under adverse circumstances such as bad weather, or a poor surface, critical spectators, noise, or fluttering plastic or paper. Imagine that this is a very important test for you. The better your capacity to concentrate, the more effectively you will be able to deal with the unexpected if your horse should react differently in some way.

• If you make a mistake, try to forget about it immediately and concentrate on the exercise or jump in front of you. Make the best of it, even if your horse does not feel right! Nor should you let yourself worry about a jump or a movement that comes a bit later in the course or test, even if it is one you are having problems with at home, because this will stop you concentrating properly on the movement you are actually doing.

Remember: The most important task is the task in hand!

5. Positive outlook and self-confidence
For every aspect of learning and performance your own motivation is the decisive factor. If you really want to achieve something you can do it, even against the highest odds! As well as motivation you need healthy self-confidence; you must make clear to yourself what you can do, and that will give you the courage to work towards the things you cannot do (yet). For example, say to yourself: 'At home I have always been able to do this, so there is no reason why I can't also do it in any other arena in the world!'

Make it a habit to express your aims in a positive way, not as what you must avoid doing, but as what it is best to do. In half-pass, for instance, don't think: 'I must not collapse my hip and let my seat slide to the outside,' but rather: 'I am sitting smoothly with the inside bend.'

Remember: Never say, 'I must not do this, I am always doing this wrong.' Instead, say firmly to yourself: 'This is how I have to do it; this is right!' The same applies to your trainer, who should never just be telling you what you are doing wrong. He will only help a pupil to progress if he gives practical hints on how to do it right.

Self-confidence, however, must never be confused with overestimation of your abilities. A self-critical attitude is essential and the goals you set yourself must be achievable: you must recognise the difference between 'I want' and 'I can', otherwise your efforts can lead to failure and this will only damage your self-confidence and motivation.

Having said that, failure (in adequate proportion!) is an essential part of every learning process. It is important to consider failure in a positive way, as the motivation for improving your performance. This can only happen if you stop looking exclusively at your mistakes, and condemning your whole performance because of them: even if you have made a serious error, consider what went well – and you will find there is more than you perhaps thought, if you are honest with yourself. Put yourself into a positive frame of mind, so that you analyse your mistakes in a matter-of-fact and productive way. In not dismissing everything out of hand you will stay more rational and will consider the more positive aspects, those that will teach you something for the future.

Ask yourself why you made this error: was it because of external circumstances, such as noisy spectators, loud music or a bad surface? Whatever it was, try to incorporate something like it into in your training programme.

Maybe you yourself were not concentrating well enough, perhaps your mental preparation was insufficient? This is something you can work on.

Did the problem lie in the horse's preparation? Perhaps he was doing exercises well at home, under perfect conditions, but they were not firmly enough established to perform reliably under test conditions? Never mind, you can practise these exercises and establish them.

Did you overtax your horse in the warm-up, maybe asked for too much, so that he lacked sparkle in the test itself? If so, you will have to think about your warm-up routine, and maybe change it.

There are many more such details that you can establish when you

analyse things sensibly, and that you can draw positive conclusions from. It is therefore all the more important to be self-confident, and not to cast doubt on all your work because of a few mistakes.

Call to mind a particularly successful day, everything that went well in it, its happy atmosphere, and this should be reason enough for you to believe in your ability to succeed.

Also find out the conditions that suit you best when you are about to start a competition: do you like things busy or peaceful? Some people don't even want to be talked to before the start, and like to use the last minutes to concentrate in total isolation. Others consider it a welcome distraction to talk to as many people as possible about anything and everything. Someone else puts on his headphones and listens to music. Yet others psyche themselves into an aggressive mood because they need a certain fighting spirit to perform at their best.

IMPORTANT It is up to you to find out the conditions that suit you best. For this, too, you need a healthy self-confidence, so that you can say to yourself: 'Regardless of what other people do or advise – for me this is best; and in the end it is up to me, and me alone, to decide what conditions I need in order to produce my very best performance.'

1.4 PREPARING FOR COMPETITIONS

You will only be successful in competitions and enjoy them, if you have considered every detail in your preparation.

• Make sure that your horse is fit enough for a competition and all that it entails, such as the time and effort needed to warm up for the test itself, maybe a second test, and sometimes a fairly long journey.

• It is a good policy to ride your horse most days in a snaffle, and to use the double bridle (where applicable) only once or twice a week, so that his mouth stays soft.

• With a horse that is lacking in competitive experience or is particularly nervous, you should try and simulate some of the conditions he will meet in competition as well as you can in the course of his training; this might include noisy spectators, fluttering plastic tape and flags, plaiting or braiding his mane, perhaps even spraying him with insect repellent. Training frequently in unfamiliar arenas has also proved to be of great benefit in a horse's preparation. Have a trial run with you and the horse dressed up in all your competition gear; he may find all this special clothing and equipment strange and upsetting, in which case try it out several times at home.

• If the horse isn't accustomed to the surface – it may be deep, slippery or uneven – it may cause him additional difficulty, so even at home try to ride on as many different types of surface as possible.

Remember: School your horse in the rain sometimes, so you know how he reacts.

• *Establish how much time you need, and the sort of work you need to give your horse when warming him up* so he gives of his best. Practise this at home. When you work this out for a competition always allow 20 or 30 minutes more; you can always include more walk intervals if the warm-up time proves to be too long.

• *Practise loading your horse* in advance, so that you allow enough time – and patience – should he be difficult on the day of the competition. Drive the route to the venue beforehand in order to avoid detours or getting lost towing the trailer, which would only make you nervous and be an additional strain on the horse.

• It is worth considering that most horses will not urinate in a trailer, which means they need to be given the time to do so after unloading.

• *Always learn the test by heart*, so that in riding it you can concentrate completely on each movement as it is required, and are not dependent on a caller to know what you are meant to be doing.

• At home, take into consideration the following points: practise the movements required in a test at different times, then put them together progressively into one session. Always use an arena with the proper lettering.

• As there is no explanation for the order of the letters in the arena, the following mnemonic may help you to remember their order, starting from M and going clockwise around the arena: 'My Best Friend Adam Keeps Every Horse Clean'.

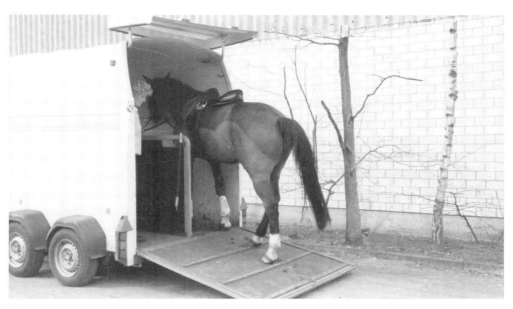

Practise loading your horse before you go to your first competition.

• Movements such as halting at X or flying changes (especially when performed on the diagonal at X in medium canter) should not be ridden too frequently on the same spot at home, because the horse may start to anticipate them or become tense and excitable. Nor should you ride a whole test all the way through too often (certainly not daily), for the same reasons.

• When you are schooling always include work on the centre line; it should be nothing special to your horse.

• Videos have proved to be of great value when assessing warm-up work and in the discussion of a whole test.

• Don't keep riding an exercise that you know is full of inaccuracies over and over again in the same training session. You will rarely improve on your mistakes that way, and it is much more likely that you and your horse will either become thoroughly bored, or tense and nervous. It is better to ride the problematic exercise now and again in between other exercises, and to be satisfied with gradual, step-by-step progress.

• Find out what puts you into a positive mood for a competition – what makes you concentrate and ready to perform? Do you need peace and quiet and no interruptions before the start, or does it suit you better to have a chat or

IMPORTANT At the competition itself, your best policy is to go through the test again in your mind in front of the arena (different spacial conception!) concentrating on its every detail. Decide where you will have to concentrate particularly (for example: here I must position my horse clearly in the corner and establish the bend for the half-pass that follows).

Try to memorise the sequence of letters in the dressage arena.

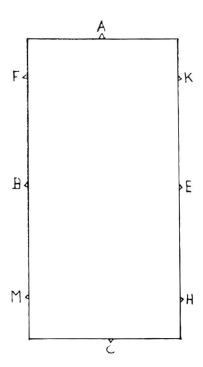

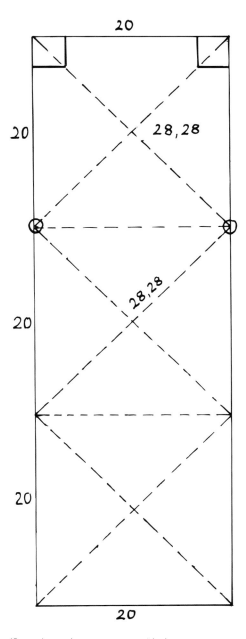

get a few more tips from your trainer?

• When actually riding the test do not provoke your horse into resisting you in your anxiety that he should perform an exercise correctly. It is better to ride the turn on the haunches, say, or the canter pirouette rather larger than to be too dogmatic and risk the horse refusing to do it at all.

• If the horse is distracted or upset by the strange environment and starts to look around, bend him slightly to the inside and ride him like this for a few strides rather than make an issue of his lack of attention. Practice and correction are all a part of your training at home; in a competition it is sometimes better not to insist on complete accuracy and submission.

Remember: Well prepared is as good as well ridden!

If you do not have an arena with the correct measurements at home, you can create one yourself: first mark a square 20 x 20m, with a diagonal of 28.28m. Then add on a second square of the same measurements for an arena of 40m in length, and for a 60m long arena add a third square.

2

BASIC TRAINING

2.1 LUNGEING

Competent lungeing is an important element of training. The first stage in a young horse's training is the work on the lunge, where he learns to establish his natural rhythm on a circle, and to become supple and balanced without being burdened with a rider's weight.

• Even young horses already working under saddle should at first not be expected to carry a rider the whole time, but should at least be lunged when warming up.

• Lungeing is also a good way of warming up an older horse before schooling him, especially if he normally starts off with a tense back or runs away from the aids.

• Lungeing can also improve horses that have problems with contact (unsteady contact, incorrect bend, resistance in the neck). It is often easier to get such horses to step up to the bridle on the lunge. The same applies to horses with a sensitive or weak back or those who become very tense in their back muscles.

• Older horses which are used to being lunged, and which you are only providing with additional exercise, can be lunged in a headcollar (halter – US). This also gives you an opportunity to observe how the horse carries himself and moves without a rider – this should indicate how effective your work in the saddle has been.

• Lungeing in a headcollar (halter – US) is also a good way of exercising horses which have an injury in the saddle-patch area.

• Lungeing as a means to improve a horse's way of going is only properly effective with the help of side-reins.

• If you cannot ride the horse yourself for health reasons, then lungeing, together with work in hand, is one way you can continue to school your horse.

Lungeing on a headcollar (halter – US).

• If your horse has not been worked for a while because of illness or injury, then you should always lunge him first, before putting a rider's weight on his back again.

• Lungeing equipment includes a lunge-line, a lunge whip, a pair of side-reins (make sure they are exactly the same length on both sides), a saddle and a bridle. You can also use a triangular (or Phillips) rein (see diagram below) instead of side-reins.

• A saddle is preferable to a roller because it stays in place better.

• The lunge whip should be long

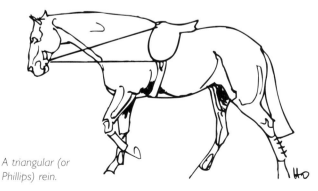

A triangular (or Phillips) rein.

enough so that you can reach the horse from the middle of the circle. If you can't, make the lunge-line shorter and walk on a small circle next to the horse. The most important thing is to maintain a constant, light contact with the horse's mouth.

• With young horses or those with a very sensitive mouth you can attach the lunge to the bit ring but also thread it through the noseband.

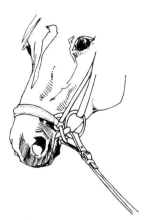

The lunge attached to the snaffle bit ring and noseband.

Remember: Run the stirrups up; dangling stirrups will only make the horse tense.

• The reins can be attached to the small ring on the front of the saddle to keep them out of the way.

• Make the side-reins long enough to keep the horse's nose in front of the vertical. Attach the side-reins at equal height towards the bottom of the sweat

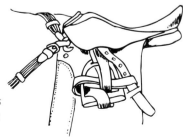

Run up the stirrups, and attach the reins to the little ring at the front.

flap; there they will be held steady by the girth straps and should stay in place.

• Make both side-reins the same length. Once the horse has reached the necessary degree of suppleness he will bend to the inside of his own accord, and then the inner side-rein will become slack.

• With an older horse, once he has stretched forwards and downwards, the side-reins can be shortened slightly. In walk you should lengthen the side-reins by one or two hand-lengths, or even better, take them off.

• For young horses you should fence off a lungeing circle if a suitable arena is not available; you can use straw bales, oil drums with poles placed on top of them, or logs; all these make good fencing-off material.

Remember: Cavaletti or jump wings are not recommended, because the horse can injure himself on their sharp corners.

• You can lunge older horses without a special lungeing circle, if they are wearing side-reins. You should regularly change the spot you use, so you do not create an uneven surface.

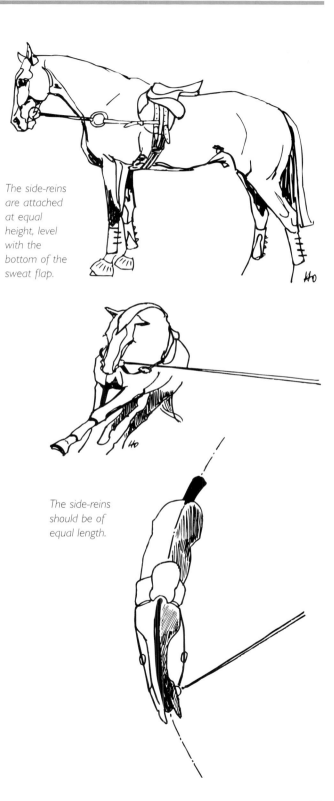

The side-reins are attached at equal height, level with the bottom of the sweat flap.

The side-reins should be of equal length.

Make a lungeing circle with bales of straw or barrels and poles.

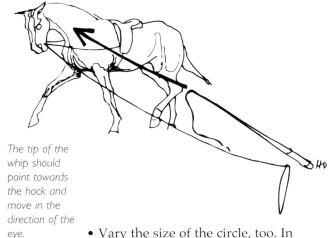

The tip of the whip should point towards the hock and move in the direction of the eye.

• Vary the size of the circle, too. In order to steady a horse that is trying to run off, or to collect him, temporarily make the circle smaller.

• It is more beneficial to walk with the horse on a small circle and to keep a soft, constant contact with his mouth than to turn him with a harsh hand on a tight circle.

• Remember to use the right technique to drive the horse on: point the tip of the whip towards the hock and move it in the direction of the eye.

• Never drive the horse faster than his own natural rhythm. Just as much as when he is being ridden, it is essential to respect his natural rhythm.

• Your voice is of the greatest importance. Never use it unnecessarily, and be consistent in the tone of voice and the words of command used.

Remember: Raising the voice will encourage the horse forwards; lowering it will steady him. Therefore raise your voice when asking for a faster pace, and lower it for a transition to a slower pace, or for a halt. Always insist that your horse reacts immediately to any

command you give him. If he doesn't respond immediately then you must quickly back up your voice with the whip. Then you repeat the command without the help of the whip.

• If your horse kicks against the whip you must use it again immediately. The principle is: the trainer always has the last word!

• Do not forget to change the rein frequently and at regular intervals.

• One way to change the rein is to halt the horse on the circle, then let him turn on the forehand. In this way you are also preparing him for the high school work which is performed in hand at a later stage in training.

Remember: Never neglect the walk on the lunge. Plenty of intervals at walk, as well as walking at the beginning and end of a session, are as important as in ridden work.

• Never ask a young horse to canter for too long; one or two circles are enough. You can improve the canter much more effectively through frequent transitions into canter.

• A horse that starts to run, or to change lead in the canter is better worked in trot for a while to calm him down. When he has regained his balance you can ask again for a transition to canter.

PROBLEMS AND TIPS

PROBLEM

The horse comes into the centre of the circle.

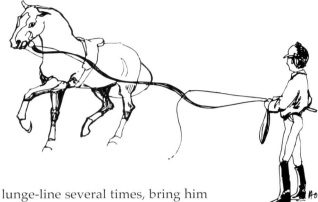

TIPS

• Drive him towards the track by making circular movements with the whip tip pointed in the direction of his eye.

• Making circular movements with the lunge-line will also encourage the horse to move towards the outside.

PROBLEM

The horse is leaning on the bit and using the side-reins as support.

TIPS

• Check the side-reins; you might have to make them longer.

• Activate the hind legs and encourage the horse to use his back more.

PROBLEM

The horse is running away.

TIPS

• Use your voice to calm him down, and by giving and taking with the

lunge-line several times, bring him down to walk. Then ask for a new transition into trot. Repeat this process until the situation is under control.

• If the horse does not respond, decrease the circle until he has to walk. Then continue the work on the original circle.

PROBLEM

The horse tries to turn and change the rein.

TIPS

• This happens mainly with young and inexperienced horses. Use your voice and the lunge-line to bring the horse

Making circular movements with the lunge-line will cause the horse to move towards the outside.

Decrease the circle until the horse is forced to walk.

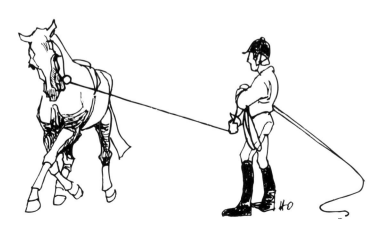

down to walk. Lead him back onto the rein he should be on, and then make sure you frame him well between the lunge-line and whip.

• Maybe get someone to help you by leading the horse.

2.2 RHYTHM IN A NATURAL OUTLINE

For the first phase of training – identified as achieving looseness (Losgelassenheit) – the following preliminary stage is vital: in a natural trot, a slightly slower pace than the working trot, the horse learns to balance himself carrying a rider in an even rhythm. He is going in his natural outline, meaning that he is carrying his head and neck freely and without shape. At this stage the horse is not yet 'losgelassen' – that is, he is not going in an extended outline with a forwards/downwards stretch and is certainly not on the bit.

First on the lunge, with very long side-reins, and later when carrying a rider, the horse learns to find a secure and calm rhythm in all three basic

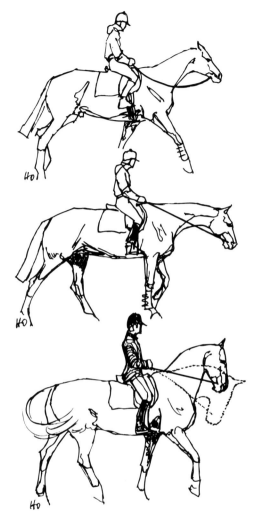

In walk on a loose or a long rein: avoid blocking him with your hand (bottom).

paces – a rhythm that can readily be observed when he is turned out or being loose-schooled.

• At this stage the work should be mainly in trot. In walk you allow your horse the rein completely, giving him total freedom in his neck. If you block him with your hand now, it can lead to loss of the ground-covering propensity in his stride and can also upset his rhythm – faults which are very hard to

Natural outline.

put right later. Do not worry about his outline in the walk. Later, when the horse is stretching towards the bit in trot and canter, he will establish an extended outline in walk all by himself.

• When your horse is secure in his trot rhythm, you can begin to improve his canter rhythm by asking for frequent transitions from trot into canter and vice versa. Avoid long stretches of canter at this stage.

• When the horse is going in his natural rhythm in trot as constantly and evenly as clockwork, then you can proceed into working trot by creating more impulsion. Only now can the real loosening work begin.

Remember: Speed must never be increased to the detriment of rhythm. If a horse starts to rush, you must slow him down; maintaining the rhythm is paramount. The same applies for many problem horses: first sort out the rhythm with the horse in his natural outline.

> **IMPORTANT** When you are warming up, allow the horse to go in his natural outline to begin with. Do not try to shape him with your hands, but keep a soft and constant contact with his mouth, and wait until the warm-up exercises help him to swing through his back when he will start stretching towards the bit by himself.

2.3 LOOSENESS (LOSGELASSENHEIT)

Looseness (Losgelassenheit) is the basis for all further demands on the horse,

no matter which particular discipline the rider is aiming for. In this state all the muscles work without tension: the circulation is stimulated, increasing the blood supply and therefore the body temperature. The horse is contented and without fear.

Looseness can only be achieved if the horse is thoroughly warmed up. No sensible human athlete would expect to achieve a good performance from a cold start!

• **Procedure:** When the horse comes out of the stable or trailer start with ten minutes at walk on a long or a loose rein. This warms the muscles and lubricates the joints. Then take up a light, rhythmical working trot, on the circle or round the whole arena. A forward-going horse can be ridden on a circle straightaway, but a lazy horse will find it easier to go large at first – circles calm the horse down, going large encourages him to go forwards.

• When you are warming up, do not ride into the corners, but ride the short side of the arena as a half circle, because at this stage the horse will not

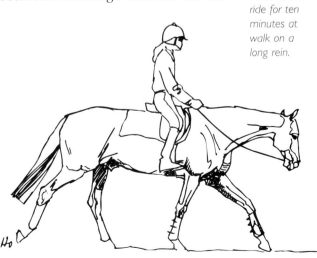

To start with, ride for ten minutes at walk on a long rein.

Horse bent on a circle.

A horse showing every sign of looseness (Los-gelassenheit).

be able to bend sufficiently to ride the corners correctly (a corner being a quarter 10m circle). Remember to change the rein regularly (every 4-5 minutes).

After a certain amount of trot work proceed to working canter, perhaps in two-point position, light in the seat.

Ride frequent transitions from canter to trot and back. Make your horse supple by bending him through large curves.

Note: Some horses warm up better in canter, so why not introduce the canter earlier and for longer? All that is really important is that you reach your aim: looseness.

• Take your horse's individual abilities and his shortcomings into account: try out the whole range of warm-up exercises. Never consider these as an end in themselves, but try to find out how your horse warms up best.

Warm-up exercises include:

• Initial period at walk

• Working trot, rising

• Bending through large curves (circles, simple loops)

• Frequent transitions from working trot to working canter and vice versa

• Warming up in an energetic working canter

• Lengthening and shortening the strides in trot and canter

• Turns on the forehand, particularly for young and problem horses

• Leg-yielding: ride this exercise with the horse's head towards the wall, or towards the centre line; ride a square, decreasing and increasing its size by using leg-yielding; ride it on a circle, as shoulder-fore

• Work over trotting poles

• Small jumps, jumping grids

• Hacking out, especially on undulating terrain

• Serpentines along a line of tree trunks

• Energetic trot or canter over open country or through woods

• Lungeing

• Loose schooling

Indications of looseness (Losgelassenheit):

• A swinging back

• The forward-downward stretch, in which the horse follows the hand of the rider forwards and downwards, seeking the bit, and in which the lowest point of stretch is when the corner of the mouth is level with the point of the shoulder

• Going rhythmically forwards without rushing

• Normal breathing and snorting

• Champing the bit with mouth closed, lightly foaming mouth

• Tail carried in a relaxed manner, swinging as a continuation of the swinging back

• Contented facial expression

Check: When you let the horse take the rein forwards and downwards onto a long rein, the horse's neck must stretch whilst maintaining a soft contact with the rider's hand.

The time it takes for a horse to become loose and supple in its way of going can vary a great deal: with a young horse achieving this state is the whole aim of the first stage of training and could take around three to five months (from when he is first backed); for horses that need reschooling, it might

be several weeks; with an older horse that is well trained, only 15-20 minutes (including the walking phase).

Warming up can take longer if:

• the weather conditions are extremely cold (when it is highly advisable to put on an exercise rug for the initial work);

• the horse has been off work for a day or longer (for example, through illness);

• the muscles are stiff from the previous day's work, or if the horse feels excessively nervous and tense.

From an extended outline the horse is gradually put onto the bit.

Extended outline.

PROBLEMS AND TIPS

In principle: You think you have done everything set out in the specialist textbooks, yet things are simply not going according to plan; in spite of all your efforts you are not getting the results you want. Below are some of the most usual problems, and tips on how to solve them.

PROBLEM

Your horse goes faster than you want.

TIPS

• Check the amount of hard food you are giving him.

• Respect his exercise requirements. In general horses are not given enough opportunity to move around. In addition to the hour they are ridden, they should have the chance of further exercise, for example at grass, either led in hand or allowed free (see page 14).

• Lunge the horse before you ride him. This is especially helpful for young horses or those in need of retraining, enabling them to relax and loosen up without the weight of a rider.

• When you ride your horse, calm him all the time with your voice, something he should be familiar with from lungeing. And try to regulate the tempo by using a sympathetic, give-and-take contact with both hands.

PROBLEM

When you are warming him up on a circle, the horse loses forwardness.

TIPS

• Don't use just the inside calf as your leg aid, but apply both calves to drive him on again.

• Go back to riding on a straight line and re-establish a good forward pace before taking up the circle again.

PROBLEM

When riding a circle you attempt to apply the inside leg to establish the bend on the inside rein – the horse's outer side stretched, the inner side hollow – but your horse will not move away from your inside leg, and perhaps even moves towards it.

TIP

• Try to 'fine tune' your horse with subtle lateral aids; for instance on the open side of the circle, say, on the right rein, make him yield to your right leg. Once he responds readily to your right leg, try once again to establish the correct bend on the right rein.

PROBLEM

The horse is not on the outside rein; his outside shoulder falls out on a circle.

TIP

• At any point on the circle, ride in a straight line, then turn through 45° and with the outside rein, straighten the horse's neck from the shoulder. Keep doing this until the problem is resolved.

The horse is escaping through the outside shoulder.

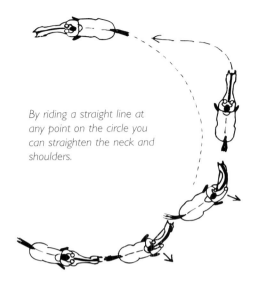

By riding a straight line at any point on the circle you can straighten the neck and shoulders.

PROBLEM

When stretching, or when asked to come on the bit, your horse overbends and comes behind the bit – as if rolling up behind it. This fault can be seen particularly in horses who are flexible through the jowl and poll, and light in the hand, and therefore have often been pulled behind the bit, which disallows the swing of the back to follow through.

TIPS

• Make sure you allow these horses to go above the bit (the natural way of going) before asking them to stretch down. Then, encourage them to stretch forwards and downwards into a low passive hand, all the while maintaining the rhythm.

• Such horses should be ridden with extremely low hands (i.e. with the knuckles of your little fingers against the horse's withers.).

PROBLEM

It takes too long for your horse to start stretching forwards and downwards with a swinging back.

TIPS

• Try out the whole repertoire of warm-up exercises so as to discover which ones are best suited to your horse to loosen him up.

Work over trotting poles can be a good warm-up exercise.

• Try working him in canter earlier and for longer, or ride frequent transitions between trot and canter.

• Use trotting poles (in walk, the distance between poles should be 70-80cm/2ft-2ft 6ins; and in trot, 120-140cm/4ft-4ft 8ins).

• Gymnastic jumping over small fences in trot and canter can have an excellent loosening effect.

• Many horses warm up and relax best on a hack; use canter, though with a light seat, and try walking and trotting over varying terrain or bending in and out through trees.

• Never force the horse into a shape with your hands; above all, concentrate on loosening up the back muscles.

• If all these efforts persistently fail to produce a good result, then have the horse examined by a veterinary surgeon to find out if there is any injury to his back.

PROBLEM

Warming up and suppling works fine

If the horse has a weak or sensitive back you should put more of your weight onto your thighs (forward seat).

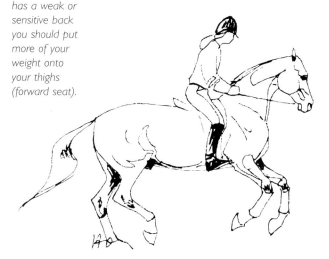

in trot, but as soon as you ask for canter and during the faster canter paces the horse tends to stiffen his back, hollows and comes above the bit.

TIPS

• Take care that you are not using your seat too actively in the transition to canter. Ride the transition as you would with a young horse, with your weight more on your thighs – the two-point position – and give the aid predominantly with your legs; once in canter sit softly and let your body swing with the movement.

Also, if the horse's canter deteriorates, through his back and in his carriage, it is worth trying the following:

• Be careful how your use your seat aids: you can only use the influence of your weight to the extent that the horse can take at the time.

• Make sure that the basics are correct in trot before trying canter again.

• Improve the canter by using frequent trot-to-canter transitions – not by long periods of cantering.

2.4 SUBMISSIVENESS (DURCHLÄSSIGKEIT)

Your horse is submissive and responsive to the aids when it works in balance and on the bit in a round outline, accepts a good contact in trot and canter, responds to half-halts promptly and willingly, and generally responds to subtly applied aids.

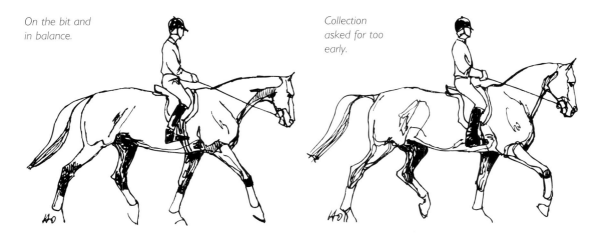

On the bit and
in balance.

Collection
asked for too
early.

(The process of taking more weight with his hindquarters and making his forehand lighter is part of full collection and is neither necessary nor possible at this stage.)

• Make sure that your horse is completely receptive to the aids before you begin any collection work. Sudden, abrupt collection after warming up can overtax the horse, leading to a tense, upside-down neck and a hollow back.

• Ride your horse from a long outline with the help of half-halts into a good

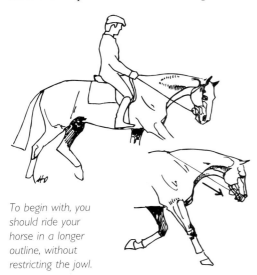

To begin with, you should ride your horse in a longer outline, without restricting the jowl.

contact so that he is on the bit, and therefore round. Depending on his stage of training and general willingness, allow your horse as much time as it needs to produce a swinging back in trot and canter on both reins (full engagement of the hocks is not required at this stage).

• When working towards submissiveness proceed as follows: start on a circle and ride your horse with a long topline (so as not to restrict the jowl) flexing him sympathetically and being careful that the poll at its highest point stays relaxed. Proceed into working trot and, maintaining a light pressure with your inside leg through to the outside rein, give and take the inside rein slowly and softly.

Check: A proper flexion is achieved if the rider, without turning his head, can just about see the horse's inner nostril and eye.

• Now with small half-halts, start making the contact more elastic and secure, constantly using your leg to move the horse into soft and never restrictive hands. To begin with, use

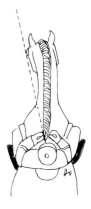

Correct flexion

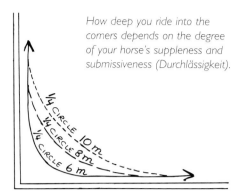

How deep you ride into the corners depends on the degree of your horse's suppleness and submissiveness (Durchlässigkeit).

By riding large curves on both reins you improve your horse's suppleness.

weight aids very sympathetically, taking into account the strength of your horse's back. Using your seat too early can spoil everything you have already achieved, because it may result in a tilted head, a hollow neck and back, and general tension.

Eventually go large, maintaining the secure contact you have previously established. Whenever contact and flexibility deteriorate, ride a half circle. Going large, make sure that you ride

the corners correctly: for this, the required quarter circle may be ridden more generously to start with (10m diameter). It is important to establish correct flexion and bend. Only when your horse has reached a higher degree of suppleness and submissiveness (Durchlässigkeit) should you ride deeper into the corners (a circle of 8m diameter and finally a volte of 6m).

> **IMPORTANT** Each corner provides an opportunity to improve contact and suppleness, but it only works if your technique is right!

Remember: The horse must be flexed in preparation to move through the corner so that the inner rein contact is light. How far before the corner you start to ask for flexion depends on the horse. A horse that can be bent around the little finger need be flexed no earlier than just before the corner, while a horse that has difficulty bending needs to be prepared several lengths before it. Once flexion is established, ride the second phase: while riding into the corner the inner leg maintains a light pressure in rhythm with the horse, and creates the bend. In the third phase you should lighten the inside rein-hand as soon as the horse reaches the middle of the corner. In the fourth, last phase ride out of the corner and straighten the horse.

Key points: Flex, bend, lighten, straighten.

• Once you have achieved the first degree of submissiveness and responsiveness to the aids in working trot, repeat the same work in working

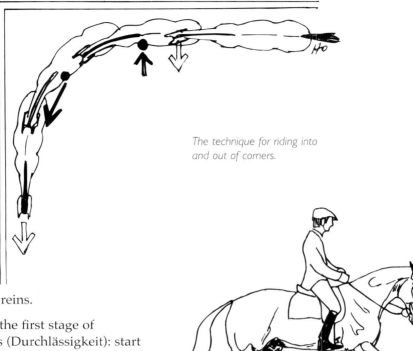

The technique for riding into and out of corners.

canter on both reins.

• **Summary** of the first stage of submissiveness (Durchlässigkeit): start on the circle, gradually working through half circles towards going large, and finally ride correct corners. With a well-trained older horse you can start riding into the corners immediately after warming up.

Check: You have established a true bend if you can give away the inside rein without the horse losing his flexion.

Check the bend: if you give with the inside rein, flexion should be maintained.

the help of the outside rein, so that his parotid glands – near the ear – have enough room and do not get pinched. Each time try again to bend him to the inside, maintaining light pressure with

PROBLEMS AND TIPS

PROBLEM

Most horses have a more difficult, stiff side. You can usually feel how the horse resists flexing on this side.

TIPS

• Repeatedly straighten the horse with

If your horse resists the inside bend, straighten him repeatedly.

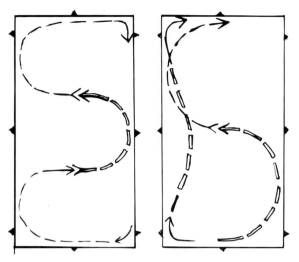

It is important to change the rein frequently.

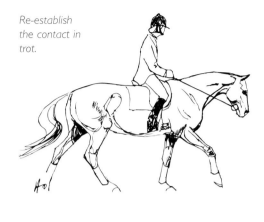

Re-establish the contact in trot.

your inside leg through to the rein. At the same time make sure that you lighten the inside rein – on no account should you try to hold onto the flexion with a rigid hand.

• Keep changing from the difficult to the easy side and back, by frequently changing the rein or riding simple loops or serpentines.

The horse is coming above the bit.

PROBLEM

My horse tends to come above the bit and hollow his neck in the transitions from working trot to walk or canter.

TIPS

• Continue in trot and re-establish the contact, then prepare for a new transition. You'll make it easier for yourself if at first you ask for the transition when the horse is on a circle and therefore already flexed and round.

• Be light with your weight aids, just as when you are warming up: you can only use your weight actively in such a measure as your horse can tolerate at his stage of training.

PROBLEM

My horse is now bending properly on the circle and is on the bit. I would like to achieve the same submissiveness on a straight line, with an even contact on both reins, but when I ride my horse straight, new problems with contact arise.

TIP

After a few strides of going straight, turn off the track and ride a half-circle: i.e. at any point ride from one long side of the arena to the opposite one on a 20m diameter half-circle. Gradually

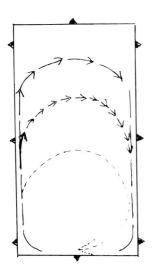

As soon as the horse shows resistance on a straight line, ride a half circle.

with the horse's mouth. Ask a good instructor to check this for you.

• You can also recognise a one-sided contact by looking at the bit – more of it will constantly be showing on one side of the horse's mouth than on the other!

• Never work the horse for too long or too intensively on his stiff side – that only leads to additional tension. Besides which, you are still working it when you change the rein because as the outside rein it must stretch in proportion to the amount of bend you ask for on the better (inside) rein.

extend the straight line until you ride the whole length of the arena. Each time the horse starts to show signs of resistance, turn onto a half-circle.

PROBLEM

The horse is supple and submissive (Durchlässig) on one rein only, for example on the left.

TIPS

• Check your hands! Often one hand is stronger and more rigid than the other, so on a straight line you feel more weight in it – it is 'jammed'. Take great care to have an exactly even contact

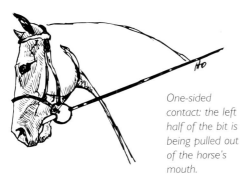

One-sided contact: the left half of the bit is being pulled out of the horse's mouth.

2.5 BASIC COLLECTION

Refining submissiveness (Durchlässigkeit)

As soon as your horse is going reliably and lightly on the bit in trot and canter, you can begin to improve his submissiveness (Durchlässigkeit) with simple collection exercises.

Simple collection exercises include:

• Transitions from working trot to medium walk and vice versa

• Transitions from working trot to medium walk (and vice versa) through four or five shortened strides

• Increasing and decreasing the strides in trot

• Transitions from working canter to medium walk and vice versa

• Straightening the horse by working him close to shoulder-fore in trot and canter

Correct half-halt.

and the rider's weight with his hindquarters, which in turn allows the half-halts to come through more easily. It is important that you execute half-halts and halts precisely in this way.

• Train yourself to feel exactly how strong or how light your aids need to be by trying out now and again how much or how little you need to use your legs, weight and hands in order to make a transition as soft and round as possible. A half-halt should never last for too long – it is better to end one with a light hand after a couple of seconds, and then introduce a new one.

Transitions from working trot to medium walk

The gymnasticising effect of this exercise lies in the fact that it encourages the horse to step further under his body with his hind legs and therefore to carry more of his

Transitions through four or five shortened strides

• Try to keep your horse in the trot rhythm for four or five shortened strides before bringing him down into walk. This is a good gymnastic exercise, and will prevent the horse from

Lengthening…

executing the transition abruptly on his own initiative, and from falling on the forehand. As soon as you feel that the horse wants to slow down into walk, use your leg to keep the trot rhythm going for another four or five strides (more, at a later stage), i.e. you determine how long the trot rhythm is maintained. Keep refining your feeling for the effectiveness of your aids by testing the horse's response again and again.

• In the same way that asking for a transition through a number of shortened strides is a useful gymnasticising exercise, so is varying the transitions. Thus on one occasion ask for a transition from trot through a few shortened strides to walk, on the next go from the shortened strides straight back into working trot; yet another time make a transition to walk at a different point in the arena.

In all these exercises you should

Varying transitions is a good collection exercise.

…and shortening are good exercises for improving collection.

Shortening and lengthening the strides.

always take care to improve impulsion (Schwung) by lengthening strides, in doing so you also exert other groups of muscles.

Changes of pace (within a gait)

• From working trot, increase the pace gradually over 10-20m. So, do not ride medium trot immediately, but to begin with lengthen the strides in trot or canter only gradually; now and again use a rounded corner or a circle. Most of all, take care to keep the rhythm exactly the same as in the working paces.

• When collecting the horse from a medium pace you should, to begin with, ride a transition to the working pace; only later in his training can you go directly into a collected pace. The most important thing is that the transitions are performed in a flexible and supple manner. Only if there is no tendency to rush can you begin to lengthen the strides from working trot to medium trot or from working canter

to medium canter. And when you ask the horse to come back and decrease his strides, make sure that, keeping the hand soft, you 'catch' the impulsion (Schwung) and maintain it in the more collected strides.

• Depending on the stage of training, this exercise can result in an expressive collected trot after only a few minutes. It is especially effective if occasionally, after getting the shortened strides, you immediately lengthen them again. On the next occasion, you should ride the shortened strides or collected pace for a little longer, say 10-20m, and then lengthen again.

> **IMPORTANT**   When increasing the paces insist that your horse responds to the subtlest of aids, stepping forwards with his hind legs immediately and energetically, so that you yourself can ride him with the smallest amount of effort possible.

Transitions from working canter to medium walk

These transitions contribute to improving the horse's submissiveness (Durchlässigkeit) in canter and introduce collection. Begin on the circle and make sure that in the transition the horse shows no resistance and stays round.

• Canter to walk transitions are of the highest gymnastic value if they are ridden with three or four canter strides before the actual transition. For the horse to do this you have to teach him gradually to keep cantering, which he will do as long as you let your legs 'breathe' with the canter rhythm: he will then keep in canter, even though his stride is much shorter before the transition. Should he come above the bit, then you must make him canter on, asking for a little more impulsion, and then re-establish the correct contact.

• Just as in the trot work, you should only practise canter to walk transitions in sensible relation to other work in canter, such as lengthening the strides from working canter into medium canter and then shortening them again to working canter.

Straightening the horse by working him close to shoulder-fore in trot and canter

In this phase of training demanding submissiveness (Durchlässigkeit) and

In the trot extensions the rhythm must remain exactly the same as in working trot. (Isabell Werth on Gigolo.)

Straighten the horse by riding close to shoulder-fore.

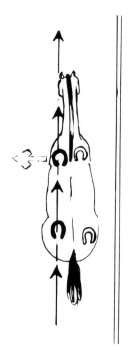

is stepping under the centre of his body and not to the side of it. It is useful to practise this at times away from the wall or fence, i.e. on the inner track, the centre line, the diagonal, in a large arena or in open country. It has also proved useful to ride diagonal lines which are different to the usual figures, and which do not lead to a change of rein: for example after the second corner of the short side of the arena you could ride a diagonal to the middle of the opposite short side (like from M to A), and then continue on the track on the same rein. Or you can ride from a point between H and B up to C or A, or vice versa.

basic collection, more attention has to be directed towards straightening the horse.

• In trot and canter you should keep thinking of shoulder-fore to encourage the inner hind leg to step forwards towards the inner fore, so that the horse

Remember: Submissiveness (Durchlässigkeit) combined with basic collection is an absolutely vital precondition for the next stage of training – the relatively higher degree of collection and the development of impulsion (Schwung).

• Only when basic collection, and the higher degree of submissiveness

Even in the highest degree of collection your horse must always be ready to stretch forwards and downwards.

(Durchlässigkeit) which results from it, have been established, can a horse's basic schooling work be considered rounded off and complete; as the first stage of training of the young horse, and the first part of every training in any discipline, it is indispensable.

> **IMPORTANT** Your horse must be ready to stretch at any time during all his work; you must be able to ride him into the forward-downward stretch at any stage, even from the highest degree of collection.

Above the bit.

PROBLEMS AND TIPS

PROBLEM

Your horse is beginning to come above the bit each time you ride a transition from working trot or canter into walk.

TIPS

• Carry on in trot or canter, re-establish the contact and then prepare for a new transition. You'll make it easier for yourself if you ask for it at first on a circle or a curve, using the horse's inside flexion to help keep him round.

• Be lighter with your weight aids, as you are when you warm-up: you can only ever use weight aids to the degree that your horse can tolerate them, which will depend upon his stage of training.

PROBLEM

Your horse is coming above the bit in the transition from walk to canter.

TIPS

• Recognise the importance of carefully prepared flexion. Put your horse temporarily into a slightly more exaggerated flexion, give him a secure contact on the outside rein and allow the first canter stride with a soft, yielding inside rein.

• If he hollows his back in spite of this, you should be more sympathetic with your weight aids. Use your weight less actively; give the canter aids more with your legs. Try to manage with less forceful aids each time.

PROBLEM

Your horse anticipates the downward transition from canter to walk, falls onto his forehand in the process, and stops.

TIP

• If that happens go back into canter immediately. To prevent the horse from stopping, it is better to allow him a few strides in trot to begin with, and make him take the weight with active hind legs.

The horse is falling onto his forehand.

IMPORTANT   Never get stuck in a rut! With persistent problems, call on any expert help possible. It is precisely because systematic basic schooling work is the absolute precondition for all other training stages that you must not make any compromises. If you can ride your horse on the bit out of the forward-downward stretch, flex him on both reins, bend him and coordinate subtle half-halts and transitions, then you have done some excellent work and you have every right to be proud of it!

CHAPTER

3

JUMPING

The purpose of including this chapter on jumping is to negate the idea that the training of a riding horse or dressage horse should only take place on the flat.

All the different elements of the horse's training complement one another. You will appreciate how, for instance, gymnastic jumping exercises can improve your horse's looseness (Losgelassenheit), and how a quiet hack in the country can affect his mental outlook.

The following notes are therefore intended to outline the sort of jumping training that can be done with almost any horse as part of his basic schooling. The exercises can also be used to improve the training of older horses.

It is not my intention to provide a complete training system for the specialist show jumper as this would be inappropriate within the concept of this book.

In the course of my work training young event horses, I have often been advised by very competent show-jumping trainers, and their knowledge forms part of the following explanations.

3.1 LOOSE JUMPING

What are the benefits of loose jumping?

Loose jumping in an indoor school is particularly useful in assessing the natural jumping ability of a horse without the influence of a rider. This is why it is often practised with horses that are for sale, for example at auctions. It is also helpful in testing the jumping ability of young horses which are not yet able to balance sufficiently under a rider.

For older horses that have finished their basic training the benefits of loose jumping are marginal, because the ways in which a horse balances with a rider and without one are fundamentally different. In any case, most problems in training over jumps

Key

Jump

Wing

Helper

Correct set-up for loose jumping in an enclosed arena.

are to do with schooling the horse under saddle (for example, riding distances correctly, shortening and lengthening the strides in canter), and these cannot be improved through loose jumping.

If you are training your horse mainly for dressage and therefore work on the flat most of the time, loose jumping can be most beneficial in providing an alternative form of exercise. You will find that it will improve your horse's looseness (Losgelassenheit), agility and suppleness, and therefore his whole performance.

Which conditions have to be fulfilled to make loose jumping an efficient exercise?

If you do not have the help of at least two, or preferably three, extra people to lead, drive and catch the horse, you are better advised not to attempt loose jumping. There is a real risk of the whole exercise degenerating into a wild chase, which would produce exactly the opposite of the desired effect, which is for the horse to be relaxed and calm. You must make sure that the horse is caught after each run down the jumping lane and then led round again to the start, as this will help keep him calm and will avoid any nervousness setting in. This also allows you to organise and change the way the fences are set up each time.

What are the considerations when building the jumps?

The best materials for the jumps are poles and planks, as these allow the heights and measurements to be varied easily according to the stage of training, and the ability of the individual horse.

• For this reason you should only use very low walls or other fillers and build the jump round these.

• Cavaletti are generally unsuitable for loose jumping because they are heavy and their end-crosses may cause injuries.

Martin Plewa showing superb style over a jump: a perfect line runs from the elbow, through the back of the hand and the rein to the horse's mouth.

• Wings are most suitable to make an inside barrier for a jumping lane; gaps should be left before and after each jump so that the helper with the whip can either drive the horse on, or prevent him from jumping the grid in the wrong direction. Wings should also be used on the other side of each jump, against the outside wall, to prevent the horse from running out and to encourage him to jump the fences in the centre.

• For safety reasons you should round off the corner where the horse is to be caught (see sketch).

• If you have only a small arena make sure that the horse has enough room in the area where he will be caught. Shorten the whole grid if necessary, or at least the distance to the first jump.

How do you construct a jumping grid for loose jumping?

The kinds of jump that you put into your grid and the way in which you position them depends on the age and stage of training of your horse.

As a basic rule you should always start with two very low jumps which your horse can manage from a quiet trot. These two jumps can be constructed as a bounce or a double with one canter stride in between, and they will serve to set the horse going in a balanced rhythm and thus encourage

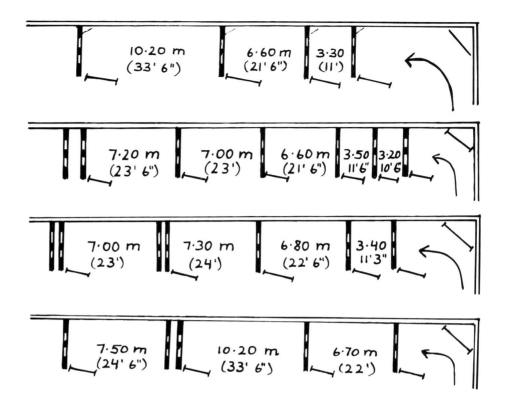

Some examples of grids for loose jumping. The distances given are approximate.

him to jump the remaining grid in fluent style. With an experienced horse you could start with a double bounce. For subsequent jumps, the following grid has proved useful, especially for young horses: add an upright fence at a distance of one canter stride, and then an oxer at two canter strides; for more experienced horses, double or treble combinations with uprights or oxers are appropriate.

> **IMPORTANT** How the grid is constructed depends on the age and training of the horse and on the purpose of the loose jumping exercises.

In theory, all the other recognised combinations used for grid-jumping, in addition to the ones mentioned above, can be built, when setting up a jumping lane.

What distances should be used in setting up the grid?
The rule is that distances in loose jumping should come as close as possible to the natural canter stride of the horse. You should therefore set the distances so that your horse can jump the fences at a calm, easy pace and without any tension or nervousness.

It is not possible to give precise measurements for the distances between jumps as you have to adjust them to each horse's individual requirements, but as a general rule we can say that for jumps up to 1.10m (3ft 6ins) in height the distance should be approximately 3-4m (10-13ft) (bounce), 6.50-7.50m (21-24ft) (one canter stride), and 10-11m (32-36ft) (two canter strides). Distances of more than two canter strides are normally not used in loose jumping. To teach the horse to judge distances he needs to be jumped under saddle.

What should the horse wear for loose jumping?

Your horse should wear a bridle with the reins removed. For leading, a rope should be looped through a coupling or lungeing strap attached to the two snaffle rings. Leading from the nearside ring alone has the disadvantage of pulling the bit through the mouth.

• Brushing boots and over-reach boots can protect your horse from injury.

How do I prepare my horse for loose jumping?

As for any other jumping work, the horse should be well warmed up before you start. So you should lunge your horse thoroughly or at least loose school him sufficiently beforehand.

Before even attempting to loose jump the horse you should give him the opportunity to get accustomed to the jumps themselves by showing them to him. This is especially necessary with young or nervous horses. By showing him the jumps the horse learns to understand what is required of him

In this jump the angle of the horse's front legs, his interested expression and his bascule are exemplary. (Martin Plewa on Habicht.)

more quickly and possible skittishness can be prevented. This usually means that additional driving with the whip, which often leads to rushed and tense jumping, can be avoided.

> **IMPORTANT** In general you should try to avoid creating any kind of fear in the horse if loose jumping is to produce the desired result – that is, to improve looseness (Losgelassenheit), agility and attentiveness in the horse.

How do I organise a loose jumping session?

For each session you will need one person to lead the horse to the first jump (for safety reasons always on the inside); at least one helper, or even better two, to hold the whips; and another to catch the horse at the end of the jumping lane.

To start with, give the horse only one fence to jump, then increase the grid step by step. You should only add to the grid if your horse has executed all the preceding exercises calmly.

The leading is done in a quiet trot. The horse should be as straight as possible, with a light but steady contact on the lead-rope. He should be released as soon as you feel that he wants to go for the jump, and never closer than one or two lengths before the first fence.

The person leading in should stand at the entry to the jumping lane until the horse is caught at the other end. Then he or she collects the horse and leads him back for another attempt at the lane.

Each time the horse jumps through the whole grid successfully, offer him a small reward (some feed or a carrot).

How do I cope with a very excitable horse?

Calm him down with your voice, hold your left hand in front of his head, and let him go very late, about one length before the jump. Some horses are controlled by occasionally halting them and turning them away from the jump.

How high and how wide should the fences be?

Specific dimensions cannot be given, because so much depends on the individual horse. In principle they should be about the same as those used when the horse is jumping grids under saddle, which would be about 60-90cm (2-3ft) for bounces, and all other fences about 90-120cm (3-4ft) in height and 100-150cm (3-5ft) in width.

A higher jump (for example, the last obstacle a grid) *should only be built if the aim is to test the jumping ability of the horse.*

> **IMPORTANT** Start with small jumps and raise them very gradually, never suddenly.

• In the case of horses that are hesitant, tense or which even refuse, always return to smaller jumps and reduce the demands on them.

• Testing the horse to his limit in each loose jumping session purely to revel in his jumping ability is unfair and unkind, and will eventually ruin his joy of jumping.

How do I finish a loose jumping session?

When the actual gymnastic jumping exercises are finished, send the horse over one final, friendly, low grid.

Afterwards the horse should be walked until he is completely calm and dry.

> **IMPORTANT** Never finish by asking the horse for his biggest exertion; always stop the loose jumping session before the horse shows any signs of tiredness.

• Never finish with a fault (a refusal or a knock-down) or an untidy jump (brushing or rapping the poles).

• Remember the calming-down phase!

3.2 JUMPING UNDER THE RIDER

What criteria have to be fulfilled before a horse should jump under saddle?

• Your horse must have learnt to respond to the driving aids promptly – for example when he is asked to move off and go into trot and canter; when he is given the collecting aids; when he is asked for a transition to a slower pace – and he must be able to accept them fairly reliably.

• Your horse should be going forwards between hand and leg with confidence and purpose, in straight lines and on large circles in trot and canter.

• Your horse should be used to stepping or jumping over one or more raised poles.

What is to be considered when building the jumps?
If your horse is already acquainted

with loose jumping you can set up the same sort of thing for the first jump training session under saddle.

Otherwise it makes sense to build the first single jumps in such a way that they can be jumped towards the gate. You should also *use building materials (poles, planks) that the horse has seen before.*

In the first phase of training it is advisable to attempt mainly small cross-poles as these facilitate the approach and encourage the horse to jump the middle of the fence.

Always use wings to start with, as a young horse's natural instinct might be to run out.

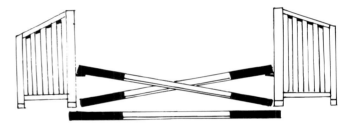

Cross-poles are especially suitable in the training of young horses.

What do I have to bear in mind when first jumping an inexperienced horse?
Only an experienced rider who can influence the horse skilfully and go smoothly with his movement, should jump an inexperienced horse.

The horse must be warmed up thoroughly but on no account should he be tired before you jump him.

• Always show your horse every new fence before you try to jump it.

• Before you tackle a new jump, keep jumping the first one until the horse takes it without hesitation in a relaxed and forward manner.

• Always approach on a straight line and try to keep to it after the jump.

• Try to maintain a *constant speed* in the trot.

Use the leg aids only to regulate the speed of the trot and to keep the horse straight. Undue pressure and exaggerated driving on are to be avoided.

• Do not try to ride your horse to a predetermined take-off point and then send him over the jump. Right from the start your horse should learn to judge the take-off independently, and to choose the ideal take-off point himself.

• Never influence the horse any more than is absolutely necessary; allow him time to direct his attention towards the jump so that he can concentrate on jumping it without fault.

Remember: The approach to the next jump starts as soon as you land after the one before!

• Praise your horse well after every jump, even after less successful ones.

• Always remain calm and relaxed yourself because only a calm and contented horse can jump in a relaxed and attentive way.

• *Avoid overwork!* Once a horse's confidence in jumping is destroyed it is not often that it can be re-established reliably.

PROBLEMS AND TIPS

PROBLEM

Your horse refuses, or jumps unwillingly or with great hesitation.

TIPS

• Jump him repeatedly behind a reliable lead horse while encouraging him with your voice and leg aids.

• For the next few days repeat the exercise several times until the horse responds reliably on his own to the voice and leg aids.

PROBLEM

Your horse is not keen to jump, and he slows down when approaching a fence.

TIPS

• Before attempting to jump again, make the horse attentive to a strong leg aid, for instance through frequent transitions from walk to trot.

• Approach in walk, and start trotting only three or four horse's lengths before the jump, encouraging the horse with your voice. Repeat this several times.

PROBLEM

Your horse rushes when approaching the jump.

TIPS

• Give him more time to warm up and more loosening work, and occasionally include a very small jump or a few trotting poles so that he learns to accept this work in trot as a matter of course.

• Try to jump more fences away from the gate.

• Include a jump on a large circle; do not use a long, straight approach.

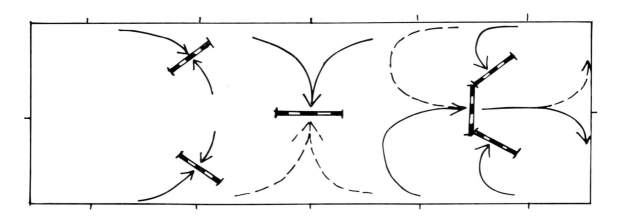

• In general do more jumping from broadly curved lines (examples for setting up the jumps are shown above).

• Try to allow the contact to become lighter and lighter as you approach the jump in order to reduce tension in the horse.

• In some cases it can even be useful to let the reins become a little longer before the jump.

> **IMPORTANT**   When you are warming up on the flat let the horse stretch down on a long rein.

With very temperamental horses it is advisable to put down a number of trotting poles (about 1.30-1.40m (4ft-4ft 6ins) apart) approximately 2.20m (7ft) before the jump (see illustration right).

• Be as quiet and secure in your seat as possible, and avoid sudden shifts of your upper body or jerky movements with your arms and hands.

PROBLEM

The horse runs away after the jump.

TIPS

• Never punish the horse or give harsh half-halts because the most common reason for this problem is that he is

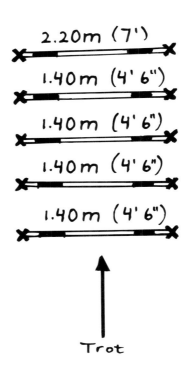

afraid of the rider's hand.

• Before the jump, only drive the horse forwards as much as is absolutely necessary.

• Use half-halts repeatedly after each jump until the desired speed is achieved; with horses that are really difficult you can use the wall in an emergency.

• When giving a half-halt from of a light seat it is necessary to sit closer to the saddle (without falling back into it) and to take your shoulders further back, if needs be into a dressage position.

• After a successful half-halt, soften the rein immediately or even lengthen it slightly.

• If the horse starts to pull again, turn him onto a small circle and bring him back to walk before moving off once more.

PROBLEM

Your horse is generally very excitable about his jumping.

TIPS

• A nervous horse should be jumped more frequently, but very little should be demanded of him.

• Your horse must learn to accept that negotiating poles and jumps is a completely normal part of his everyday work. That is why you should include the occasional small jump from trot in your daily work.

• Even dressage training should take place frequently in an arena that contains jumps.

• With nervous horses, *maintaining a constant speed and rhythm* is of particular importance. Avoid sudden changes of speed!

• Try as hard as you can to achieve an especially still, secure seat and a calm way of giving your aids.

• Frequent hacking out will generally improve the horse's mental attitude.

PROBLEM

Your horse resists the aids, leans uncontrollably against the hand and finally runs out.

TIPS

• First consider if you have overworked your horse – maybe you have jumped him too high or too often.

• Try to ride your horse with a very light contact as you approach the jump, because the most common reason for this problem is that the rider is heavy-handed.

• To achieve a soft contact without losing control, it often helps to ride with the reins held wider apart as this lessens the pressure of the bit on the horse's mouth. Many horses are more easily positioned this way, and soon stop resisting the rider's hand.

• Approach the jump in as quiet a pace as possible so that you are better able to soften your rein contact.

• The height of the jump should be appropriate for the speed.

• Give several short half-halts, always

in conjunction with a 'giving' rein aid, to prevent the horse from taking the bit between his teeth when approaching the jump.

• Bending the horse, or changing the bend several times before the jump, can be helpful.

• In many cases, jumping on a curved line, or just as you leave one, makes correction easier.

• Never use either extreme pressure or severe restraint when approaching a jump, because the horse will want to fight to free himself at the first opportunity.

Take care never to provoke resistance or induce obstinacy!

PROBLEM

Your horse will not approach a jump straight.

TIPS

• First of all, when working your horse on the flat practise straightening exercises which are appropriate to his stage of training, in order to try and avoid the problem altogether.

• In order to correct this fault it is helpful if the horse has already learnt to respond to the lateral leg aids; this means that you will be able to prevent him veering to one side with appropriate leg aids.

• Jumping cross-poles makes it easier for the horse to learn to take the jump in a straight line and in the centre.

• By putting down poles to make a lane leading into a jump you can create a kind of 'funnel', which is especially useful for young and inexperienced horses.

• If the horse constantly deviates from a straight approach to one side in particular, the cause may stem from the fact that most horses are naturally stiff on one side (crooked).

• If the horse is stiff to the right, you should jump him more often from a left bend, or approach the jump with the horse positioned to the left by your strong inside leg. If the horse is crooked to the left, the opposite applies.

PROBLEM

Your horse jumps diagonally across the jump rather than straight through the middle.

In principle: The cause of this problem is because the horse is not straight and

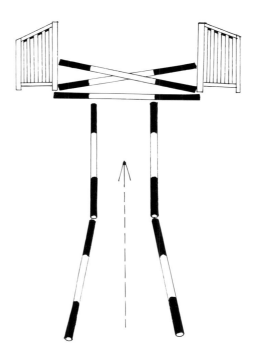

Layout of poles in a 'funnel' in front of the jump to practise a straight approach.

therefore the hindquarters do not carry the weight evenly in the take-off phase: it is often the result of the rider collapsing one hip as he jumps, a common fault.

TIPS

• Check and correct your seat over a jump. Always stay centred on the horse – the weight you feel in each foot in the stirrup should be equal.

• Try to improve your horse's straightness on the flat.

• With a horse that always jumps to the left, approach on a left circle and jump the fence at an almost 45° angle, positioning the horse away from the direction he would jump towards. If he jumps to the right, approach on the right rein.

• Do not make the angle too sharp because it could encourage the horse to run out to the opposite side.

Possible correction method for a horse jumping crookedly: an additional pole is placed diagonally for a horse that is crooked to the right and trying to run out to the left.

• In some cases it can prove successful to raise the height of a cross-pole on one side only or to add a pole which is put up on just one side (see illustration above).

• It also often helps to lay a guide pole in front and on top of the middle of the jump, as shown in the sketch above right.

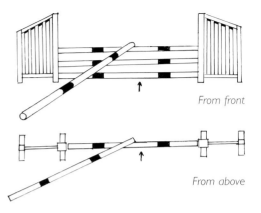

From front

From above

Another possible correction method for the same problem as shown below left, but in this case a pole is placed on the middle of the top pole.

PROBLEM

The horse is tense and hollows his back while jumping.

TIPS

• Check if your horse is sufficiently loosened up (losgelassen) on the flat; if he is not, increase the warm-up time.

• Practise 'giving away the rein' frequently, repeating it several times, in both trot and canter; this encourages the horse's looseness (Losgelassenheit) and his trust in the rider's hand, and it is also the best preparatory exercise for the development of the bascule. The 'giving away' of the rein on the flat corresponds to the allowing rein over a jump, and the forward-downward stretch is the precondition for the necessary rounding of the horse's back over a jump.

• A good exercise is to hack over undulating ground or small hills, since this uses all the strands of muscles that are most needed in order for a horse to bascule over his fences and in a relaxed and supple way; they are worked in a manner similar to the way they would when the horse is jumping.

• Any exercises which improve the lateral bend of your horse will also improve the way he uses his back, because one or other of the two bands of muscles along the spine will be activated and strengthened.

> **IMPORTANT** Take care how you use your hands: the rider's hand must neither be completely rigid and block the horse, nor should it give up the contact altogether by suddenly going forwards.

• With horses that have back problems a light seat is very important, even more so in the landing phase. (Additional advice on how to improve the horse's back and his manner of jumping can be found in the next section, Gymnastic Jumping p.70).

PROBLEM

The horse is jumping carelessly and keeps hitting the poles.

TIPS

• First try to find the cause of the problem. If the horse is tired, let him have a break, and after a small and successfully jumped fence, finish the work immediately.

• For the good of the horse's training in the long term, you should never finish work on a badly executed jump.

• If your horse still has difficulties in

finding the right take-off point and in developing the correct parabola for a clean jump, put down a pole to mark the ideal take-off (approximately 2-2.30m (6-7ft) before the jump if coming in trot).

• If the way the horse tucks up his legs could still be improved, keep the demands low but with carefully structured exercises, help him to develop better technique, athletic ability and quickness of reaction (see also section 3.3, p.70).

• Your horse must be given a one hundred per cent chance to clear every

> **IMPORTANT** In training, never cause the horse to hit the poles (by rapping) or to knock them down!

jump, so as a matter of principle try to avoid knocking any down, and any other faults too.

• Always approach a jump steadily, otherwise you will make your horse apprehensive.

• Your horse should never be afraid of a jump.

• Never punish the horse with your hand, through abrupt half-halts, or with the whip or spurs for any mistakes, because he will never connect rapping or knocking down a pole with the punishment; he will only become frightened, nervous and tense.

• Your horse reacts to fear and insecurity just like you: he will make even more mistakes!

• If your horse starts to lose concentration, you must make sure that you avoid monotony in his work: so do not jump the same fence too frequently, and change the type of jump more often.

• You can also direct your horses's attention back to a jump by changing its appearance; even small alterations may be effective, such as putting cones underneath it or a rug on top of it.

• At times surprise the horse by approaching a jump when he least expects it, e.g. straight after a tight bend or immediately after a short break.

• Try to change location as often as possible, and jump your horse in other, unfamiliar arenas.

Additional ways of improving your horse's jumping technique and concentration can be found in connection with the gymnastic exercises for jumping, in section 3.3.

Small cross-country fences help to develop the horse's trust and agility.

How often should I jump my horse?

There is no answer that can apply to every horse; how often depends on the age of the horse, the demands of his training and what he is to be used for.

A horse that is to be trained for show jumping or eventing should be worked over jumps three or four times a week, and for the eventer, cross-country jumping will be part of that training.

A riding or dressage horse can and should do gymnastic jumping exercises once or twice a week.

Horses that are still very inexperienced or nervous should be jumped somewhat more often, but with fewer jumps per session. With such horses the inclusion of jumps or trotting poles must become a normal part of their everyday work.

Note: Negotiating small obstacles from trot can hardly be considered as jumping.

In time the horse must progress to coping with higher demands. Careful but regular work over fences will keep him fit and healthy, so that later he is able to cope with show-jumping competitions and cross-country events, to go hunting, also to tolerate a more rigorous level of dressage training and stay fit and sound for years to come.

3.3   GYMNASTIC JUMPING

Every jump, even a single one, should in theory help make your horse more gymnastic in his work on the flat, and therefore develop and improve his elasticity and suppleness, build up his muscles and improve his co-ordination. However, the *gymnasticising effect* can be further increased if grids (such as used in loose jumping) with varying distances are included in dressage training. You can begin training over combinations when your horse has learned to jump small, single fences in a straight line and with confidence.

The criteria for the rider apply in the same way as for work over single jumps: for example he must be able to maintain cadence and rhythm, and to judge the right speed; he must develop the horse's sensitivity to the aids, and be able to keep him between hand and leg on a desired line; and he must know the conditions for building the fences properly. (See also section 3.2.)

How do I build up a grid?
A *step-by-step* approach is recommended, as follows:

• In front of the first element of the grid put down a trotting pole at a distance of 2-2.20m (6-7ft). The horse will remember this from jumping single fences out of trot.

• This exercise can be extended by placing another trotting pole about 3-3.50m (10-11ft) behind the jump.

• The distance depends on the height of the fence and the length of the horse's canter stride.

• Once the horse has completed this simple exercise several times the next jump in the grid can be added, at a distance of about 6-6.50m (20-21ft) from the first fence.

• By using this method of building up the grid – alternating between fences and elements on the ground – you can

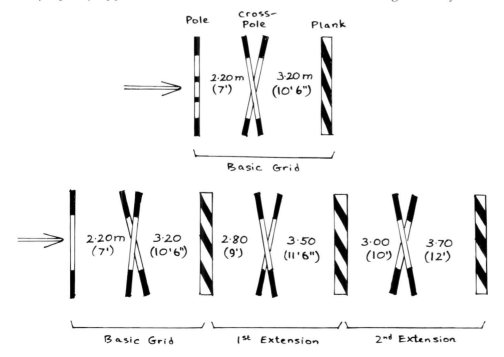

Setting up a jumping lane (distances given are approximate).

extend it step by step (see illustrations on the previous page).

Remember: The distances can become slightly longer as the grid becomes longer.

Experience has shown that in this way horses learn more easily and quickly how to jump a row of fences in a straight, fluent and rhythmical manner, because their attention is always needed for the next jump. Thus they are not tempted to try and avoid the aids by not keeping straight, or to run out, or to become too fast and rush through the whole grid. Gradually some of the ground poles can be removed and the distances changed to two or three canter strides.

How often do I jump a grid?
As often as it takes the horse to jump the grid as a matter of course, in a relaxed (losgelassen), fluent and rhythmical manner.

If possible not so often that the horse loses his concentration and starts to jump hurriedly and carelessly.

Never so often as to tire the horse.

Remember: Horses, like people, learn by repetition.

In order to establish fluency and the desired style of jumping in gymnastic jump training it is necessary to consolidate any improvement the horse makes with plenty of practice, although still being very careful not to overdo things, either mentally or physically.

Having to make several jumping efforts in a short distance, as in a grid, clearly puts a greater strain on the horse than does jumping a single fence. For this reason the horse, particularly the novice, must be allowed to get used to it little by little, and the training should be organised in a progressively constructive way.

• Try to make jumping lessons interesting and instructive for your horse by introducing change and varying the exercises.

• Endeavour to exercise the whole horse gymnastically and to enhance all his talents and abilities.

• Work on your horse's good points as well as on his problems.

• Always allow your horse short breaks so he can relax, and so his mind can register what he has achieved.

3.3.1 SELECTED GYMNASTIC JUMPING EXERCISES FOR BASIC TRAINING

In this section I will outline what I consider to be the most useful jumping exercises, and why; from my point of view these have proved to be of most value in the training of horses up to the level of ability where they can jump (the German) standard fault- and-style jumping competitions successfully.

All the exercises assume that the horse has been thoroughly warmed up and prepared in his work.

Exercises for the improvement of balance and rhythm
Schooling for rhythm begins on the flat

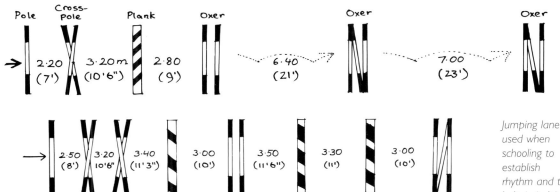

Jumping lane used when schooling to establish rhythm and to help in judging distances; approach the top lane in trot and the lower lane in canter.

by way of the exercises and methods that train and confirm rhythm and balance, such as half-halts, changes of rein and work over trotting poles.

Remember: A frequent cause of loss of rhythm is the wrong basic speed.

• Therefore try to find the right basic speed both for your horse and for each fence or combination and keep to it.

• When approaching a jump *avoid any abrupt driving on or shortening up of the horse.*

• Do not upset your horse's balance by suddenly changing the length of the canter stride; allow him to concentrate on the jump and the right take-off spot.

It often helps to ride for a while in the basic speed that is thought to be appropriate for a jump, before even approaching it, in order to acquire a feel for that speed.

Gymnastic jumping is particularly useful in developing the rider's feel for rhythm. For that purpose we recommend longer grids with several small elements, which should be put up at optimal distances most suitable for the horse.

Essentially the overall rhythm will be determined by the first elements, therefore the first jump of the grid should help the horse find that rhythm: place a trotting pole in front of it if approaching in trot, or set it up as an easy bounce if approaching in canter.

• With distances of more than one canter stride, elements on the ground between the jumps, such as trotting poles or slightly raised poles, can help to establish the rhythm.

• The construction of the fences should be inviting – for example, build oxers with only a narrow spread or upright jumps with their groundline brought forward.

• You should set distances which, when tackled at the right speed, entail the rider having to influence the horse very little.

• Strictly avoid any unnecessary driving on or half-halts.

Remember: Any loss of rhythm is the rider's fault! If the rider is responsible for upsetting the horse's rhythm, further jumping problems will ensue, such as knocking jumps down, tension, loss of confidence, excitability, other difficulties of rider control, and failure to judge distances and point of take-off.

Exercises for improving the bascule and use of the back

As already described in section 3.2, you should place particular emphasis on *loosening work* before you start any jump training.

Frequent changes between a more collected dressage-type carriage and a longer, lower (extended) posture, frequent allowing of the rein in all three paces, as well as exercises which improve the lateral bend (for example turns, shoulder-in and suchlike) all enhance the use of the back muscles and the elasticity of the neck muscles, which are of central importance to the horse rounding his back and stretching his neck over a jump. Again I would like to reiterate the value of work whilst out hacking, especially riding over undulating terrain (no mountaineering!) with the horse on a light contact and in a lower outline, in all three gaits but in a quiet pace. Such work is very effective in strengthening and activating the muscles which are needed to make a nice bascule over a jump.

> **IMPORTANT** Experience has shown that in order to achieve the desired extended outline many gross mistakes are made, often through the misuse of aids like draw-reins. An extended outline is the result of the horse stretching forwards and downwards, following the giving rein but without losing the contact.

• Even in this lower outline your horse should step forwards to the bit on a soft contact and without leaning on it.

• This means that your horse must stay in balance, even in the extended outline; he must not fall onto his forehand and drag his hind legs.

• In this lower outline you often have to drive the horse forwards to a greater degree.

• If your horse is pushing downwards against the hand, ride on a circle and increase the inside bend for a short stretch, then slowly lengthen the rein, using the release of the inside flexion to encourage the horse to take the bit forwards and downwards without snatching it out of your hand.

• If the horse tosses his head about it is usually a sign that the rider's hands are too hard and the contact is too strong; always try to ride with a soft contact.

• The forward-downward stretch can be achieved more easily if, while on a circle, you take your inner rein clearly away from the withers. A wider manner of holding the reins decreases the pressure of the bit on the horse's mouth, and makes it easier for the horse, even a very sensitive one, to find the way down.

Remember: Every time you force a lower outline with your hands or with auxiliary reins you achieve only the opposite of looseness (Losgelassenheit).

If you apply force to lower the head your horse will react with counter pressure – he will use his under-neck muscle to resist the rein or auxiliary rein. The result will be an increase in tension in his back, and a strengthening of all the muscles that are positively disadvantageous for jumping.

Pulling the horse's neck down will also lead to the horse becoming unbalanced and falling more onto the forehand. Thus it will be more difficult to keep his hindquarters active, the croup comes even higher and in spite of the low neck, the back cannot swing.

Many horses avoid a forced contact by coming behind the bit, and go along with their nose on their chest and usually with a 'break' in the neck (when the poll is not the highest point). Again, the activity of the back is impaired, not enhanced.

Take care: Not every low position of the head and neck adopted by your horse means that you have achieved the forward-downward stretch! The stretching of the neck must start, just like a properly executed jump, at the withers, and this is the only way the back can be rounded. Any forced low outline is counter-productive!

• In all jump training you must make sure that you go with the movement of the horse, that you take your weight off his back and always establish a soft contact; a blocking hand that pulls backwards, a heavy seat or being behind the movement all prevent the horse from developing a good bascule.

• As you approach a fence, strive to encourage the horse to stretch his neck; try to push the rein forwards towards the horse's mouth with your hands held low, though without losing the contact completely. With many horses it is helpful to hold the reins wider apart.

• It is wrong to force the horse into a low outline before a jump, because he will only try to free himself upwards by tossing his head and will thereby hollow his back.

Remember: Before you attempt any special grid exercises aimed at improving the horse's bascule, prepare him by jumping several single jumps and bounces from trot.

In the gymnastic grid illustrated below, three small oxers follow each other at a distance of one canter stride each. (This grid could also be built with a maximum of four small oxers.)

Distances and sizes should initially be easy and inviting, to allow completely tension-free jumping without any great exertion. The demands are increased gradually in such a way that the first oxers are slightly increased in height and then slowly widened from the front, so that the distances between jumps are reduced.

Shorter distances, and small but slightly wider oxers, make the horse

A jumping lane for improving the horse's bascule (distances given are approximate).

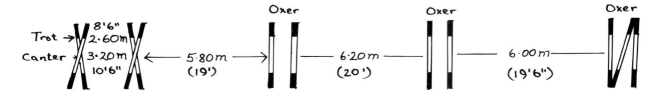

bring his hind legs more underneath his body and stretch his topline more over the jump. The effect on the muscles in the back and quarters brought about by these shorter distances combined with spreads is comparable to compressing and then releasing a flat spring.

To develop the rounding of the back in the first half of the horse's effort over a jump, a bounce with a higher second element is recommended for many horses. Maximum extension of the topline, especially in connection with a stronger use of the hindquarters at take-off and on landing, can be achieved by work up and down steps (see illustration below).

Cross-country exercise for improving activity of the back by achieving maximum stretching of the topline.

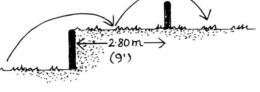

This considered, it is lamentable that natural jumps such as banks and steps have disappeared from most show-jumping courses.

Some trainers suggest that you leave a bandage fluttering behind a jump or place a diagonal pole on top of an oxer to make the horse look down at the jump and so improve his bascule; however, I do not favour such methods of training as they which rely entirely on optical effects, and because they treat the symptom, not the cause. Also such effects, in my experience, lose their impact very quickly.

> **IMPORTANT** You cannot force a bascule!

• Raise your demands slowly; overtaxing the horse is counter-productive.

• *Concentrate on your seat and your aids,* particularly on going smoothly with the horse's rhythm in a light seat and maintaining a soft contact.

Exercises to improve the judging of take-off

The aim of jump training in basic training *must be,* that your horse learns *to judge the correct point of take-off independently, and learns to cover the distances between fences in the appropriate basic speed and with a rhythmical approach.* Depending on your horse's ability, you will have to employ appropriate exercises that either make him keener to jump, or make him approach the jump with a greater degree of collection.

With slightly *hesitant horses who lose impulsion in the approach,* and also those with a short stride, you should try to *improve obedience and sensitivity to the aids in your preparatory work,* for example by changing pace more often, by frequent but short spells of driving him on from a working pace, and by using more transitions from trot into canter.

The quality of the canter stride is best improved out hacking; regular canter work at a forward show-jumping pace is recommended for every riding horse.

• The single fences at the beginning of a schooling session should already be jumped from canter, and the first jump into a jumping lane should be ridden in canter, too.

• At first, measure the distances to suit your horse, then later pull them out slightly. The distances between jumps should be set up for two or three, sometimes even four canter strides (approximately 9.80-10.50m (32-34ft), 14-14.60m (45-48ft) or 17.50-17.80m (57-58ft) respectively), so that, if necessary, you can drive your horse forwards more effectively between jumps.

• For horses that jump hesitantly, bounces should at first be avoided.

The profile of the jumps should be really inviting to make your horse jump fluently, and to encourage him to stretch over the jump in good style; an example grid is shown overleaf.

With horses that hesitate, the contact with the mouth may well have to be slightly stronger – as long as this is achieved with stronger leg aids and not merely with the reins.

Take care that any driving on is done only with leg aids.

I personally consider it a fault to sit down in the saddle and use strong, active weight aids, often in conjunction with too much movement in the upper body; this style can often be observed in riders before and in between jumps, and I feel it must be disturbing for the horse.

To get a horse used to shorter distances and to train him to shorten himself up before a jump, even when he is travelling at greater speed or in a longer stride, you should make sure that in his dressage work you place particular emphasis on submission

Only with good basic training and a horse's complete trust in his rider can such jumps be tackled with confidence.

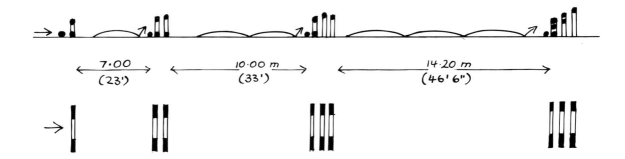

Example of a jumping lane suitable for improving technique in horses who jump hesitantly (distances given are approximate).

(Durchlässigkeit) through the use of half-halts and transitions.

If collection and half-halts do not work on the flat, they are even less likely to be successful when jumping.

Practise half-halts, and also shortening the canter strides, from a light (two-point) seat and with shortened stirrups. To execute a half-halt from a light seat, the rider takes his upper body back slightly, he sits closer to the saddle, and his middle swings forwards and downwards in rhythm with the collecting rein aids.

Practising smooth transitions between the light seat and then sitting back with shortened stirrups, is an excellent exercise to prepare yourself for executing half-halts.

> **IMPORTANT** Avoid giving half-halts with just the reins because you are standing in the stirrups. Correct this fault by taking your feet out of the stirrups for a short moment in order to give the half-halt.

Depending on the horse's stage of training you should include *easy collection exercises, for instance voltes (6m circles) in canter,* in your dressage work.

Riding transitions while hacking out over small hills or undulating terrain can assist your collected work in an effective way: when riding uphill the muscles in the quarters are strengthened, and when riding downhill half-halts and halts lead to an increased bend in the haunches, greater engagement of the hind legs and a strengthening in their carrying power; the horse's ability to collect is therefore improved.

In jumping work with horses that are over-keen or have a very long canter stride, a very quiet, almost passive seat is of the utmost importance; any sudden movements of your upper body will speed your horse on even more.

• Make sure that the aids to collect the horse after the jump are applied in time, that is just before landing, and also straighten your upper body slightly earlier.

• Half-halts between jumps must only be brief, and must always be followed by an allowing rein.

• To make the jumps look more striking to the eye, use fewer poles, and materials such as planks and solid fillers, which may help to slow the horse down.

If the horse starts to rush while

jumping a full grid, it is better to take him over several different, shorter grids.

Remember: Do not practise the same exercise too often.

• As a rule, commence with a bounce and make the subsequent distances single canter strides, because the problem of canter strides that are too long or that are rushed only gets worse with greater distances.

• Bounces in the middle or towards the end of the grid also help to reduce the horse's speed (an example for this set-up can be found below).

• To start with, use trotting or canter poles between the jumps.

• Try to shorten the canter stride by bringing the groundline forwards (use a trotting pole or small filler element), and later reduce the whole distance between the two jumps. In the course of his training your horse has to learn to negotiate distances of less than 6m (20ft) without difficulty.

Many horses learn to 'come back to their rider', if poles are placed on the jump in such a way that the horse jumps into a sharp angle (see illustration above right).

Remember: In order to pick up a horse

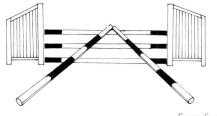

Possible fence arrangement to correct a horse who jumps flat.

From front

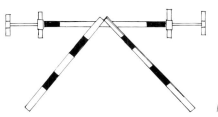

From above

that is not coming back to you, always start by trying to shorten the canter strides. See if you can influence your horse by using trotting poles and groundlines brought forwards before you shorten distances. Introduce half-halts early enough; never try to give them too close to the jump!

3.3.2 FURTHER EXERCISES TO IMPROVE THE HORSE'S JUMPING TECHNIQUE

You have to assume that not all shortcomings in jumping technique can be remedied; the natural talent of

Example of a jumping lane that should help to correct horses who rush into jumps.

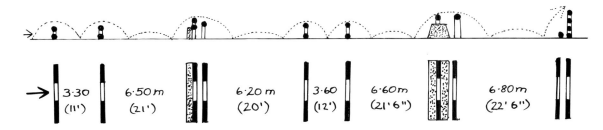

| 3·30 (11') | 6·50 m (21') | | 6·20 m (20') | 3·60 (12') | 6·60m (21' 6") | | 6·80m (22' 6") |

many horses is limited, and in turn this limits the extent to which their jumping can be improved; then again, other horses are so naturally talented for jumping that many gymnastic exercises, especially those for jumping technique, are superfluous. Up to this point we have described and explained jumping exercises that should always be part of the basic training of any horse, even in the training of a future dressage horse. They are calculated to fulfil the basic requirements for jumping fences, and to help overcome the most common problems and difficulties that can ensue; but they only concern the jumping of fairly small fences as they are generally used in basic training.

Should you want to improve your horse's jumping further, because you want to jump him in higher classes for instance, then you will have to improve your horse's jumping technique as much as his natural ability will allow. Setting out a full training programme for the specialised jumping horse is not the intention here, but we will mention a few well-tried practices for the improvement of jumping technique.

Exercises to improve foreleg technique

• Try to improve the agility and strength of the horse's limbs, for example by hillwork, transitions, lateral work, trotting poles.

• Aim to ride closer to the groundline; if necessary mark it with a trotting pole.

You can achieve a similar effect with a bounce where the second element is higher.

• In combinations containing an oxer the latter can be built with a slightly higher front; also the distances in a combination should be gradually reduced.

• If the horse tucks his front legs under unevenly, try jumping him more often out of tighter turns or at a sharper angle – though take care not to tempt him into running out.

• The reasons for the horse not bending his forelegs enough, especially at the point of shoulder and in the elbow joint, are similar to those for not using his back, the same exercises therefore apply (see section 3.3.1).

Exercises to improve hind leg technique

The agility and flexibility of the hindquarters can be improved with hillwork, trotting poles and such like, and also with exercises such as half-pirouettes in walk, rein-back and lateral work.

• Try to jump with the horse in greater collection; bad hind leg technique usually results from an insufficient degree of collection and activity of the hindquarters.

• For this, suitable jumping exercises might include: bounces with a slightly higher first element, as well as bounces that contain small spreads.

Gymnastic jumping grids should contain several spreads with the front pole higher in one, and the back pole higher in the next, and so on alternately.

Remember: In jumping exercises which include a number of spread fences, extra care is required not to overtax the horse, because his confidence can easily be destroyed that way!

Exercises to improve the power of the hindquarters

The ability of the horse to jump well depends on the development of a good engine in the hindquarters; therefore all exercises that strengthen and activate the hindquarters are beneficial, for example transitions, combining collection and lengthening exercises, halting and moving off on an uphill slope etc.

• The classic exercise to develop spring (muscle-power) is the bounce, and its beneficial effect can be increased by setting up a row of bounces.

• Spreads jumped off tight turns or from a closer distance are also suitable.

• When you ride across country you can further improve spring by schooling over uphill combinations, for example steps or stairs.

Exercises to improve quickness of reaction

Quickness of reaction is generally instilled by very varied, all-round work, part of which should include riding frequently in unfamiliar arenas and hacking out in different areas of the country.

• In jump training, the materials for the jumps should be changed as much as possible.

• It is also effective to keep changing the distances in a grid.

• With horses that are slow to respond, grids should be ridden at a faster basic speed.

• Responsiveness is also developed by jumping in unusual situations, and by jumping several different, small courses, with short breaks in between.

Remember: Gymnastic jumping should be a vital part of every horse's basic training, regardless of what that horse will become later; in pure dressage, jumping training constantly complements and balances the work on the flat, while in specialised jump training it will gradually be replaced by the training for a particular standard of show-jumping course.

Gymnastic jumping must never become a strain on the horse; the great value of such exercises lies in the fact that a high degree of gymnastic ability can be achieved with low demands and small jumps.

The exercises shown in the illustrations should only be considered as examples, as standard exercises which you can use to design and set up new variations of gymnastic grids.

Remember: Variety is good both for you and your horse!

In all the variety and specificity of jumping exercises, the limit should be where the construction is unfair to the horse and might cause him to make mistakes. Exercises that undermine a horse's confidence achieve the very opposite of the beneficial results that properly conducted gymnastic jumping can bring.

• You should also use gymnastic jumping for your own training, most of all to improve your seat and balance through exercises such as jumping without reins or stirrups, and to school your feeling for distances and rhythm.

3.4 TIPS FOR FURTHER JUMP TRAINING

The aim of any jump training is that the horse successfully completes a jumping course that corresponds with its stage of training; the best way to check if your training is going the right way is to go out and jump a course of that standard. Thus, as soon as you feel the horse is ready to jump such a show-jumping course, you can set up and practise fences of the required

Such evident confidence is only possible with thorough basic training. (Thies Kaspareit on Sherry.)

dimensions at regular intervals, for instance every two weeks, and gradually make them more difficult. The criteria of most show-jumping courses are above all contained in the exercises that demand obedience and responsiveness, such as transitions and distances. That is why we recommend schooling the horse first on the flat and then over short sections of a show-jumping course, in order to ensure that the required submissiveness for a whole course is guaranteed.

The measurements of the fences are of importance insofar as they influence the distances; thus when the fences are small, the distances must be kept in the lower regions of the accepted measurements for striding. We advise every rider to use a tape measure when setting out the distances between jumps

and in combinations, and to walk them as well in order to acquire a feeling for distances. This experience will serve you well when you have to walk show-jumping courses in unfamiliar arenas or at competitions. And you can assume that any horse which has been carefully and expertly introduced to jumping, and which has also had regular and efficient gymnastic jump schooling in addition to his dressage training, can manage a certain standard of course in a satisfactory manner.

In practice, problems arise in spite of all this, and not only in jumping, problems for which there seem to be no solutions offered in theory and literature. In fact the theory can only provide the equipment for the practice; it cannot replace the rider's feeling, which can only be gained through years of working with horses. If you try to use the tips offered here for jump training like recipes in a cookery book, you are in danger of totally misunderstanding the training of the horse, and of considering it merely as a system of subjugation for certain ends. Rather, you have to look at every horse as an individual, with his very own physical and mental disposition. To recognise those characteristics and to structure the training accordingly distinguishes the good rider and trainer. For this reason our practical tips for jump training are only meant to be suggestions: it is your responsibility to put them into efficient practice.

4

PACES AND SIMPLE MOVEMENTS

4.1 THE BASIC GAITS

4.1.1 THE WALK

Walk is a gait that can only be improved very slightly by training. Therefore a future dressage or event horse should have a fairly good walk to start with. In some dressage tests the walk is counted double (the mark is multiplied by two).

Criteria for a good walk:
– It should cover a lot of ground: the hind foot should touch the ground as far as possible in front of the imprint of the front foot on the same side. It is desirable that the front legs should stride out freely from the shoulder.

– As important as the amount of ground covered is an established four-time footfall: the horse should step forwards diagonally with one foot after the other clearly visible on each side, but never at the same time. You can judge if the footfall is likely to be regular and correct because if it is, a clear 'triangle' is formed by the front leg that is just about to step forwards, the hind leg on the same side and the horse's belly.

– Forwardness is primarily achieved by driving the horse on properly.

• Drive the horse on in the four-beat rhythm, using each leg alternately: this means you apply each leg aid exactly at the moment the hind foot leaves the ground.

• If you have difficulties in finding the right rhythm for your driving aids, take your feet out of the stirrups and let your legs hang loose. Like this, you will feel them fall against the horse's sides alternately all by themselves, and this is the rhythm you want.

• Consider the following four points, and you will have no problems with the walk:

1. In medium and extended walk

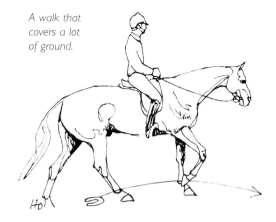

A walk that covers a lot of ground.

always make the reins one or two handwidths longer than in trot or canter. Allow the frame of the horse to extend significantly, but keep the neck under control.

2. Make sure your shoulder and elbow joints are relaxed and loose so as to allow the natural nodding of the horse's head. Do not block it with your hands.

3. Never attempt to overcome problems with contact in walk. For this, the paces with more impulsion – trot and canter – should be used. If you have made your horse submissive (durchlässig) in these two paces, then he will be on the bit in

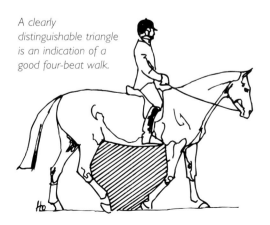

A clearly distinguishable triangle is an indication of a good four-beat walk.

walk, too.

The walk is also a quite unsuitable pace for correcting any other resistance or disobedience. Such problems are best sorted out in a more clearly forward pace, in trot or canter.

4. At the beginning and end of each training session, and in the rest intervals, you should ride at walk on a long rein.

Walk on a long rein.

• If the horse becomes restless or starts to jog when you shorten the reins, overcome this by constantly changing the length of the reins in the walk intervals, so that the horse does not automatically associate shortening the reins with a transition into trot or canter.

• You can improve the reach of stride somewhat by frequently walking the horse on deeper going or over or poles.

• In competitions it is tactically prudent to make no great difference between medium and extended walk, but simply to show the maximum length of stride possible. In the extended walk you merely increase the feeling of diligence and purpose.

The walk should be rhythmical with the stride covering plenty of ground.

• A *pacing walk* can be corrected by generally improving looseness and submissiveness, and by strictly adhering to the four points mentioned above.

• For the *collected walk* shorten the reins, keep your hands in that position with flexible, elastic wrists, and keep driving the horse forwards in the four-beat rhythm so that the strides become shorter and more elevated, but not slower than in medium or extended walk.

Take care: Even later in training do not practise collected walk for too long or too often, and always ride it in conjunction with medium or extended walk. Otherwise you can easily ruin the length of the horse's stride in extensions, or even the rhythm.

Pacing walk.

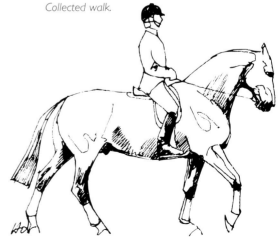

Collected walk.

• Many horses go unlevel, and some even 'pace', in collected walk. If this is the case, you will achieve a better result in competition if you ride the collected walk more freely, towards medium walk, rather than risk faults incorrect rhythm, for which ultimately you will be penalised twice because the final mark for purity of the paces will also be affected.

4.1.2 THE TROT

• *The trot is the gait that can be improved most successfully through training.* By developing the carrying power of the hindquarters, the shoulder becomes freer and more expressive, and so also does the trot.

Criteria for a good trot:
– A clear *two-beat* footfall, that must stay the same in all tempi – that is to say it must not become slower or faster in rhythm.

– *Plenty of impulsion* (Schwung) from behind; the hind legs should be stepping under the body as far as possible. As a rule of thumb, in working trot the hind foot should touch down on the hoof print of the front foot.

• With a young horse, first ensure that you have established a natural, unhurried rhythm, before you ask for more impulsion in the working trot.

• Even with an older horse if it is rushing in trot, first re-establish this natural rhythm at not too strong a pace.

Take care: In the extensions the rhythm must be strictly maintained – it must not become faster.

• In the collected trot, too, the rhythm must remain the same – it must not become slower or sluggish.

• With horses that tend to hurry the rhythm in extensions, the following procedure has proved to be successful: in rising trot, gradually (never suddenly!) lengthen the stride a little, and maintain that increase, keeping precisely the same rhythm, for half a circle or for the long side of the arena. Then lengthen the stride a little more, and again establish rhythm and balance.

As you do this, be sure to round the corners well, and keep increasing the stride and re-establishing the rhythm until gradually you reach medium trot. Do not forget to change the rein regularly!

Only when your horse stays secure in his rhythm in rising trot, and his back keeps swinging, can you change to sitting trot – and then only as long as his rhythm and back stay right.

In trot the horse springs from one diagonal pair of legs to the other.

• When riding a horse with a *sensitive back* it is best to alternate between rising and sitting trot, even after the warming-up and loosening phase. This means: if your horse is starting to get worse in sitting trot then, go back immediately to rising trot. Neither you nor the horse's back will benefit from sitting trot if the horse's back is tense!

• School your horse so that just the very lightest of leg and weight aids will keep him in medium or extended trot until you give the restraining aids.

• Should the horse start to rush, for example on the diagonal, then ride the trot extensions on a different line, and also through rounded corners or on a circle.

Remember: Trot is the working gait per se. It is the easiest for your horse, because each moment of suspension results from the moment of support provided by each diagonal pair of legs, in turn: it is therefore a pace full of impulsion because the horse always has two feet on the ground to carry and balance himself and his rider.

This is why, after the initial period at walk, stage you normally begin a training session with warming up and suppling exercises in trot: it applies to every session, and also throughout the horse's whole training. Stiffness, tension, problems with contact and other instances of resistance are easiest to correct in trot.

Facing page: The trot must have a clear two-beat rhythm which stays the same in the extensions. (Herbert Rehbein on Robby.)

An excellent extended trot. (Karin Rehbein on Donnerhall.)

A canter, just as it should be – round and 'uphill'. Nicole Uphoff-Becker on Rembrandt.

4.1.3 THE CANTER

The canter, like the walk, is a gait that can be improved only marginally by training.

Criteria for a good canter:
– We want the canter *round* and *uphill*, in a clear three-beat rhythm with a distinct moment of suspension, and well balanced.

– When the horse is running free (loose) look out for good flying changes – although the exceptions to this proviso should not be disregarded altogether: there are horses which hardly show a proper change at all when running free, and which under a rider have learnt flying changes without any problems.

– In general, horses with a long back have more difficulties with the canter, and in the collected canter particularly.

> **IMPORTANT** You can never improve the canter by cantering for long periods, but only through frequent transitions. Transitions from trot to canter constitute a very good loosening exercise. Transitions from walk to canter have a good collecting effect, but it is important that the horse 'jumps' into the first canter stride in a round and harmonious manner.

• With horses that come above the bit in the strike-off into canter, remember after the initial rising trot to assume sitting trot for the last few strides before you ask for canter strike-off: in doing so, you will avoid any sudden impact of weight on the horse's back, such as can be the consequence of the canter aids.

• Avoid too deep a seat in transitions into canter; put your weight more onto your thighs, and sit smoothly with every canter stride. This also applies to horses with a *sensitive back*, when performing suppling exercises in canter. Use the light, two-point seat!

• Horses with a very good canter, which loosen up better in canter, can certainly be cantered earlier on in a session.

Take care: Horses which at the beginning of a lesson offer a very settled canter with a high croup, must be ridden more forwards.

• Riding energetically forwards in canter has an excellent suppling effect: the increased stepping-under of the hind legs causes the long back muscle to contract and thus stimulates the activity of the back.

A good canter stride.

If a horse has back problems try not to sit in too deeply.

• **Walk-to-canter transitions help to improve collection in canter,** but here, too, it is advisable to sit lightly if the horse is coming above the bit. Take care to make the strike-off round and fluent.

• In training, in the downward transitions from canter to walk or to halt you can quite happily allow a few strides of trot in between. The most important thing is that the horse allows your half-halts to come through.

Riding energetically forwards in canter makes the horse's back more active.

• **Practise making your canter aids more co-ordinated and subtle.** They are

harmonious if you can feel how they correspond to your seat in each canter stride. Make yourself aware of this by consciously feeling your aids with each stride.

• An older horse which has been taught flying changes recognises the first indication for canter strike-off as coming from the rider's outside leg. Remember, though, that a young horse is made to strike off in response to your inside leg.

• You will make it easier for your horse to understand when you want a transition from canter to trot, and when you want one from canter to walk or halt, if you make your aids different in the following way: in the downward transition from canter to trot, bring the outside leg more forwards into its normal position; in the downward transition to walk or halt keep your outside leg in the canter position.

4.2   THE HALT

In the halt in its correct form the horse should be standing absolutely still, square, on the bit and straight.

• The young horse, however, must first learn to stop and to stand calmly; the other criteria are initially disregarded

Remember: Standing still is practised first; after that, work towards achieving the halt in its correct form.

• **You should teach a young horse the halt in hand to start with.** Lead him on the left rein on the track, ask him to stand with a soft pull on the rein and a simultaneous voice aid, for example

'Staaand!, then ask him with an encouraging 'Walk on!' to walk on again, and repeat this several times. It is less important which commands you use, as long as you always use the same words in the same tone of voice. Your horse will soon respond to the voice aid alone. Insist patiently but consistently that on your command he stands perfectly still, and praise him when he does.

• For horses that become unruly when being led, a special 'chain leader' (see illustration) is recommended. It has a small chain which you put over the bridge of the nose and thus any pressure is put on this rather than on the horse's mouth.

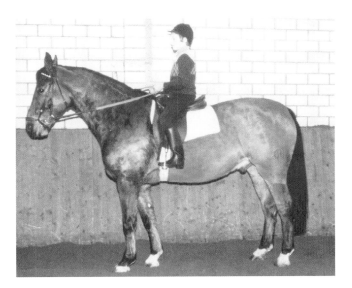

To begin with, the young horse must learn to stand in a relaxed and natural manner.

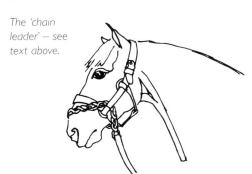

The 'chain leader' – see text above.

• In the work on the lunge you should also make sure that the horse responds to the same voice aid and stands absolutely still. Only then should you approach him and change the rein.

• *Mounting* provides another good opportunity to practise the halt. Your horse must learn to stand still obediently whilst you get on, take up the reins and put your right foot in the stirrup, and if necessary adjust the length of your stirrup leathers. He must not move off until you have given him the aids to do so. Try to be

absolutely consistent in this matter, too. It not only makes it easier to teach the correct halt later on, but it might also be helpful in avoiding potentially dangerous situations.

• *Obedience training* should not be limited to schooling under saddle. It should begin in the stable, for example when grooming and hosing the legs. It

A correct halt.

is not that difficult to train your horse so that eventfully he will stand still without being tied up.

• When riding, use every opportunity during the walk intervals to halt the horse quietly and to get him used to it, even on a long rein.

• Only when this is going well should you start teaching him the correct form of the halt: on the bit, square and straight. If he is not standing square, for instance if his right hind leg is trailing, you should ask him with your right leg to make it step under; but do not give too strong an aid, otherwise the other hind leg will be left behind. Restrain him from stepping forwards with both hands. However, at this stage do not take accuracy too far – a little lassitude is tolerated even in a test.

• *If your horse's halt is not straight, you should repeat the downward transition to halt,* making sure that you are keeping him well between your legs and maybe putting him into a slight shoulder-fore position.

• Check your horse's halt in a mirror or ask somebody on the ground to check it for you. If you keep turning round to check yourself, you will make the horse restless.

• If you are practising for a competition, it is advisable to ride further than the required point for halt, otherwise your horse will start to anticipate the downward transitions and stop on his own initiative.

• If a transition from canter to halt is asked for, it is better to ride the transition through a few strides of trot and to allow the horse's hind legs to step smoothly under his body, rather than to put him onto his forehand. This will also make it easier to achieve a square halt.

• *A last tip for the upward transition halt to trot:* in your training, teach the horse to move off straight into trot, using plenty of impulsion (Schwung). Down the centre line you can move at a slightly more forward pace to prevent the horse wandering or being crooked.

4.3   TURN AROUND THE FOREHAND

The turn around the forehand is a suppling exercise and serves to teach the young horse and the young rider the effect of the lateral aids, or to make them clear again to a problem horse. The rider then uses the different forms of leg yielding to continue practising the lateral (or sideways-driving) aids.

• Understanding the effect of the lateral aids (the horse moves away from the inner leg) is a precondition for all loosening or suppling work on large curved lines.

Hosing down the horse's legs: even if he is not tied up, he should have learnt to stand absolutely quietly.

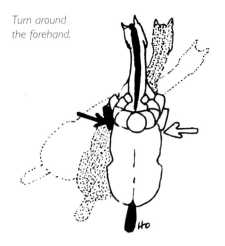

*Turn around
the forehand.*

• In *practising the turn on the forehand*
you should allow the horse's front legs
to step around on a small circle at first.
Start with one step – that is, you let the
horse step over once, with front and
back legs, then make him square up
and halt, and praise him as soon as he
has responded to your aids. Then ask
for two steps, halt again and praise him
again. Your outside leg and rein work
to restrain and support the horse on the
outside.

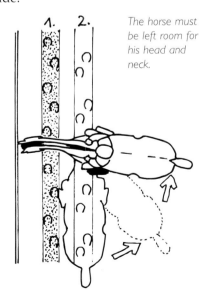

*The horse must
be left room for
his head and
neck.*

• At this stage it is not important for
the horse to be on the bit; the aim is for
him to learn to understand exactly
what the sideways-driving leg aid
means, since it constitutes the basis for
all loosening and suppling work.

Take care: After applying initial
pressure with the inside leg, you
should relax it again; try not to be
applying it constantly. Memorise this
short maxim: *Pressure, step, relax.*

• In an indoor arena, ride 5 metres
inside the track for a turn on the
forehand – after all, your horse needs
some room for his head and neck.

• In a correctly performed turn around
the forehand the horse should be on the
bit, bent round what will become your
inside leg (the one that is giving the
sideways-driving aid), and he should
make enough sideways steps with his
hind legs to perform a turn of 180°
while stepping on the spot with his
front legs.

PROBLEMS AND TIPS

PROBLEM

**The horse does not respond to your
inside leg.**

TIPS

• Support your inside leg with the
whip just behind it.

• Control the flexion.

PROBLEM

Your horse steps forwards.

TIPS

• Restrain him with the outside rein.

• Control your outside leg. It should only be supporting and controlling the quarters. If it is pressing at the same time as the inside leg it will be giving a forward-driving aid.

4.4   LEG-YIELDING

The basis for leg-yielding should be the turn around the forehand. Leg-yielding is also a suppling exercise and is mainly useful in establishing and refining the lateral aids, and thus in preparing the horse for bending work.

Procedure: The horse is flexed towards the sideways-driving leg. Take care to support the sideways movement with the outside rein, so that the horse cannot fall out onto his outside shoulder.

• *The angle in leg-yielding should never be sharper than 45°:* your horse must have enough room for the inner hind foot to cross over, so that it does not kick against the opposite coronet!

• Never ride the exercise for longer than about 20 metres or half a long side or circle. Then ride forwards in walk again, and repeat the exercise when it becomes necessary.

• During leg-yielding you should be driving the horse on with alternate leg aids in the walk rhythm, but make sure that you are getting through with your inside leg.

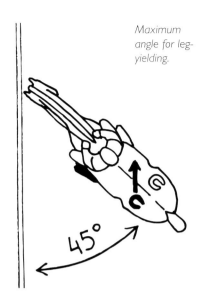

Maximum angle for leg-yielding.

Remember: Your horse must really be crossing over. Apply your aids each time one of the hind feet is lifting off the ground.

• If your horse is not yielding to the inside leg promptly enough, you can use the whip close behind your calves or the spur to support your aid. What is most important is that afterwards you

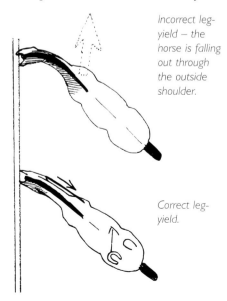

Incorrect leg-yield – the horse is falling out through the outside shoulder.

Correct leg-yield.

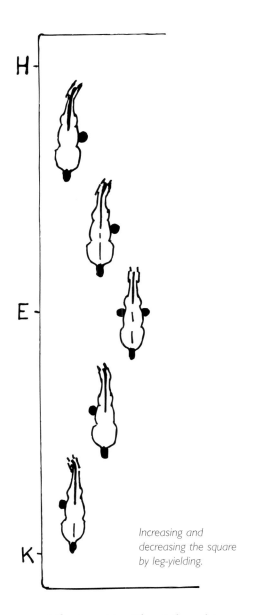

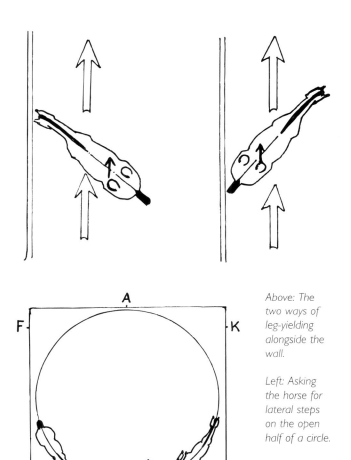

Above: The two ways of leg-yielding alongside the wall.

Left: Asking the horse for lateral steps on the open half of a circle.

Increasing and decreasing the square by leg-yielding.

repeat the leg aid without the whip or spur and insist on an immediate response; in other words that you are continuing to teach your horse to respond to increasingly subtle aids.

• *There are four different forms of leg-yielding.* The first and easiest is the one where the horse is leg-yielding on the track, with his head towards the wall.

In the second one he is going with his head towards the inside of the arena.

• In the exercise that we call 'increasing and decreasing the square' you leg-yield from the first corner of the long side, starting at the letter, parallel to the track towards the inside of the arena until you have reached the point in the middle between the track and X (5 metres each side). There you straighten the horse, and then flex him towards the new sideways-driving leg. At the letter before the next corner you come back onto the track.

• One of the most difficult exercises, but also the most effective, is to leg-yield on the open half of a circle. It is very useful for making your horse sensitive to your inside leg, so that later your inside leg will be more effective in the subsequent bending work on the circle. Therefore you should be making your horse responsive to the inside leg on the rein on which you are planning to work on the inside bend.

PROBLEMS AND TIPS

PROBLEM

The horse is bent too much in the neck and is falling out over the outside shoulder.

TIPS

• Support the neck close to the shoulder by subtly opening and closing your outside hand.

• Straighten the neck, and ride straight for a few lengths, then begin a new leg-yielding exercise.

PROBLEM

The horse does not yield sufficiently to your inside leg.

TIPS

• Make sure he is sufficiently prepared by performing a turn around the forehand.

• Drive the horse on with alternating leg aids in the rhythm of the pace.

• Support the inside leg for a moment with the whip or spur.

PROBLEM

The horse is stopping, and he is not crossing over in the rhythm of the pace.

TIPS

• Check that you are giving the aids in the rhythm of the pace, and at the same moment as each hind foot leaves the ground.

• Do not make the angle to the wall sharper than 45°.

• Start off the leg-yielding in a forward walk.

4.5 THE REIN-BACK

Conditions: Before you start practising the rein-back, the horse's submissiveness (Durchlässigkeit) must have advanced far enough, so that he is performing downward transitions from trot to walk and to halt smoothly. He should be able to do transitions within trot, and to execute a correct halt, on the bit and square.

The aids: Apply the same aids as for moving off, but then do not allow with your hands: softly catch the forward movement and let the horse push himself off backwards. With the very first step become light with your hands.

• Repeat these aids with every step but more lightly.

Remember: The most important thing is never to start the rein-back by pulling the horse backwards with the reins –

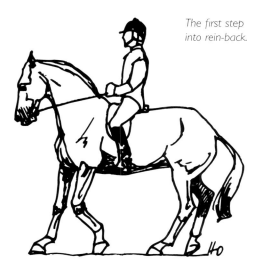

The first step into rein-back.

Finish the rein-back with half a step.

avoid doing this, and you will not have any serious problems with rein-back.

• As soon as the horse responds with half a step, immediately praise him.

• *Do not sit too deeply to start with, but be light on the horse's bac*k by shifting your weight slightly more onto your thighs. Keep the horse evenly between your legs to keep him straight.

• If any resistance occurs, first bring the horse back to a light contact on the bit. Then apply the aids again, asking for another rein-back at the moment you feel the hind legs start to move. Only when the horse will execute one step with complete submissiveness (Durchlässigkeit) should you ask for further steps backwards.

• A correct rein-back should be dead straight, with the horse on the bit, submissive (durchlässig) and his legs stepping back in diagonal pairs. In order to complete the movement with a square halt you should end the rein-back with half a step.

• A more advanced movement which evolves from the rein-back and is performed later in training is the '*Schaukel*' (the 'rocker'), which is an excellent means of improving and checking submissiveness (Durchlässigkeit), the bend through the haunches and the carrying capacity of the quarters.

• A very good exercise to improve submissiveness (Durchlässigkeit) and collection is the transition into trot or

To begin with, take your weight off the horse's back slightly.

In rein-back the horse should walk backwards with regular steps, his legs moving in diagonal pairs.

canter straight out of rein-back.

• *Vary the number of steps in the rein-back*, so that the horse neither anticipates the movement nor stops on his own initiative.

PROBLEMS AND TIPS

PROBLEM

Your horse does not step back in a straight line, he deviates to one side, usually the right. This is also a frequent cause for irregular steps.

TIPS

• Take your leg back by about one hand's breadth on whichever side he deviates in order to keep the horse straight on that side.

• Use the wall as an additional support – thus if the horse is falling out to the right, rein back on the left rein on the track.

PROBLEM

Your horse comes above the bit as he begins, or during the rein-back.

TIPS

• Stop the exercise immediately and put him back on the bit.

• To prevent the horse coming above the bit during the rein-back you can lower his head and neck slightly more to start with.

• Be careful with your weight aids!

PROBLEM

Your horse is not stepping backwards diagonally, his croup is too high and his haunches are not bent.

TIPS

• Move off again, and activate the hindquarters first in a forward pace.

• With the help of transitions and by increasing and decreasing the strides in each pace, you should strive to make the horse submissive (durchlässig) again.

• Then ask for the first steps of rein-back from a clearly forward inclination.

PROBLEM

Your horse comes above the bit in the transition into trot or canter from rein-back, or is showing stiffness.

TIPS

• Re-establish submissiveness (Durchlässigkeit) with other exercises.

• Be more sympathetic with your weight aids.

4.6 TURN ON THE HAUNCHES AND HALF PIROUETTES IN WALK

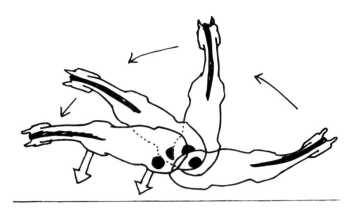

• In the turn on the haunches and the half pirouette in walk the horse steps in a clear walk rhythm (four-beat!) in as small a circle as possible round his inside hind foot. The turn is finished at 180° and you should ride the last two steps in half-pass manner back to the track.

• Take special care that the inside hind foot steps towards the horse's centre of gravity – that is, on no account should it turn on the spot.

• You may check the inside hind foot now and again by looking down while executing the turn.

• Remember to drive the horse on with alternate leg aids as in walk; don't concentrate solely on your outside leg; and most of all, use your inside leg to activate the inside hind foot. This way you also keep the horse from deviating to the inside.

Remember: It is better to turn on a slightly bigger circle than for the inside hind foot to twist or to stay still temporarily.

• The turn on the haunches, like the rein-back, should also be introduced with a half step forward. With the inside rein, lead the forehand towards the inside, then relax the rein again.

• When you first practise this movement you will have to pay particular attention to the forward tendency. At first ride a so-called *working pirouette*, in which the hind legs step around a circle of about 80cm (2ft 6ins).

• Later you can ride this working pirouette either once, or once round and back again. This is an excellent exercise to stimulate the activity of the inside hind leg: your horse is learning to step round with it rhythmically.

• Only when this rhythmical stepping round of the hind feet is established

Turn on the haunches, or half pirouette in walk.

The inside hind foot must step round rhythmically.

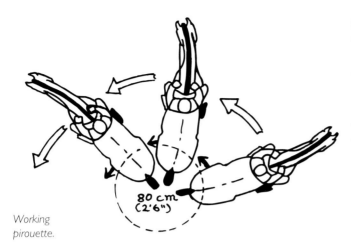

Working pirouette.

80 cm (2'6")

to your outside leg or even deviates to the outside.

TIPS

• Make sure your weight falls towards the inside; the horse will want to step under your weight.

• Make him responsive to the outside leg with exercises such as decreasing the circle.

• Take the whip in your outside hand, and when necessary support your outside leg with it.

• Make sure that you are allowing your horse's neck to flex with the outside rein, and are therefore giving him room to step round the bigger circle on the outside.

PROBLEM

Your horse's inside hind foot is not stepping round rhythmically.

TIPS

• Go back to practising the working pirouette regularly.

• Check that you are giving the sideways-driving aid alternately in the rhythm of the walk.

• Check whether you are allowing the inside rein to become lighter each time you lead the forehand sideways.

should you *gradually* decrease the size of the pirouette.

• Here is another possibility: ride the beginning of the turn, that is several steps, and then proceed straight ahead. Perform this quarter pirouette, then follow it with the half pirouette, several times. In this way you prevent the horse from crossing over behind.

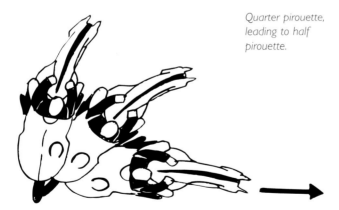

Quarter pirouette, leading to half pirouette.

PROBLEMS AND TIPS

PROBLEM

Your horse does not react sufficiently

4.7 COUNTER CANTER

The basis for counter canter round corners and on the circle must be the collected canter.

• You can start practising as soon as your horse's working canter is in balance, and he can perform a transition from walk to canter in response to subtle aids.

• The following sequence of exercises has proved to be very effective in developing counter canter on a straight line:

– Start in trot, for example on the right rein, and begin to ride a loop on the long side; one or two lengths after leaving the track, make a transition into left canter – then make a downward transition to trot again one or two lengths before reaching the track, and as you get to the track, canter on the true lead through both corners.

– On the following long side, change the canter lead via a few strides of trot at the same points. Repeat this several times, until your horse strikes off in response to subtle aids and stays in balance.

– Should your horse become worried and tense, it is best to carry on in true canter after trying a loop for half a circuit or so.

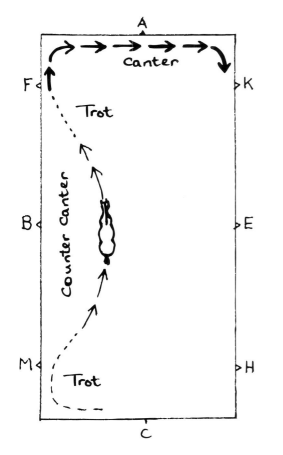

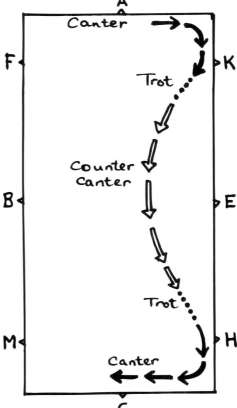

Far left: Developing counter canter on simple loops.

Left: Simple change of leg in canter through a few strides in trot.

In counter canter the horse should not be flexed any more than in true canter.

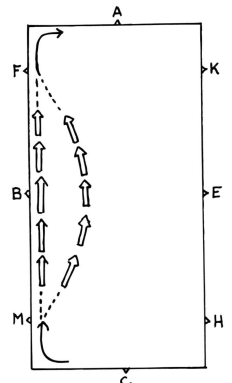

Make the loop increasingly shallow until finally you ride counter canter on the track.

– Gradually make the loop more shallow, until you are riding counter canter on a straight line.

• If you have any experience in teaching a horse flying changes, then this is the time for the first flying change: the counter canter is not yet established, and your horse's natural inclination is still to change to the true lead. So you are practising counter canter and flying changes at the same time.

• The most important *tips for the aids* are these:

– Take care to position your legs precisely, in order to make it as clear as possible to your horse that you want him to stay in counter canter.

– Support your horse on the outside rein, and ease the inside rein to let

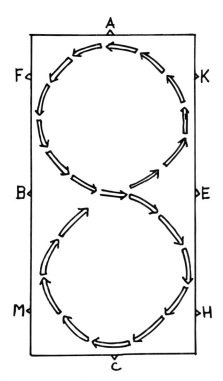

Figure of eight with counter canter.

the strides flow.

– Do not ask for more flexion than in canter on the true lead, so that you are not blocking the inside hind foot.

– Remember that your weight, just like in true canter, must be slightly more on the inside seat bone.

• Only when the horse can manage counter canter on a straight line, should you continue it first through one, then through two corners. Clearly round off the corners to begin with, and do not forget to praise your horse when he has understood the exercise.

• The most difficult form of counter canter is the figure of eight in counter canter: you should therefore ask for this last.

• Never ride in counter canter for too long, and remember to go back to true canter regularly to regain impulsion (Schwung).

PROBLEMS AND TIPS

PROBLEM

Your horse is going crooked – that is, he is moving on two tracks, usually to the right.

TIPS

• Correct this by riding close to shoulder-fore on the appropriate rein (thus in counter canter on the right, ride shoulder-fore right).

• Lengthen the strides slightly.

PROBLEM

The horse changes the canter lead.

TIPS

• Calmly make a downward transition to trot, then a new transition into counter canter.

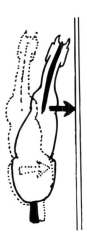

Straightening the horse by riding close to shoulder-fore.

105

• Never punish the horse! You do not want to stop the horse doing flying changes.

• Make sure you have sufficient collection and submissiveness (Durchlässigkeit).

• Go back to riding counter canter in its easier form, for instance with very shallow corners.

• If your horse is changing canter lead in the exercise 'Change of rein on a short diagonal, without change of canter lead', then you have probably been riding too sharp an angle to B (or E respectively): you should try instead to ride the angle much flatter, especially when you first practise the exercise.

PROBLEM

Your horse starts to run and fall on his forehand.

TIPS

• Establish a sufficient degree of collection by practising walk-canter transitions in true canter.

• Establish the counter canter with simple exercises, such as on shallow loops (see above) or on the straight, before riding the corners.

• Should the horse start to lose collection in counter canter, make a downward transition straightaway, then ask for a new transition into counter canter.

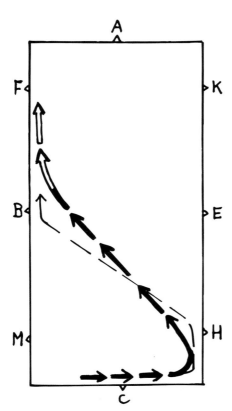

Ride a shallow angle when changing the rein on the short diagonal.

CHAPTER

5

WORKING TO ADVANCED LEVEL

5.1   WORK IN HAND

The purpose of work in hand is to gymnasticise the horse without the additional burden of the rider's weight.

• The horse learns to bend his haunches, to step under his centre of gravity and to push himself up off the hand (bit), which means he becomes altogether more responsive.

• Lazy horses can be made more active through work in hand – excitable, sensitive horses can be calmed down.

• It is also easier to overcome the effect of bad conformation with work in hand (for example, too long a back or an unfavourable angle of the hindquarters).

• Work in hand is also another way of being able to continue to work the horse if he has an injury in the saddle area but can be worked in a roller, or if the trainer cannot ride the horse for health reasons (for example because he has groin strain or back problems).

• *A horse should only start work in hand if he has been expertly lunged and has learned to move laterally round his handler on a volte in walk.* You can start teaching him this lateral movement in walk as soon as he shows every sign of looseness (Losgelassenheit).

• Before embarking upon more advanced work in hand it is essential to have completed the horse's basic training (see Basic schooling work, p.19).

Take care: Before you begin any work in hand the horse must be properly warmed up, either on the lunge or under a rider.

• The *equipment* is the same as when riding the horse, though in place of a saddle a roller can be used (nevertheless check that it cannot slip and chafe the horse).

• If the horse is wearing a saddle you should buckle the side-reins level with the middle of the saddle flap or the end

Making the horse move laterally around you on a volte.

of the girth straps.

• In addition to the aforementioned equipment you will need a special whip for work in hand, about 1.50-2m (5-6ft) long. Brushing boots or bandages can prevent injuries. To begin with, side-reins, a lunge-rein and a lungeing whip are very much recommended.

• In place of side-reins the so-called triangular (or Phillips) rein (see illustration below) can be used.

• When your horse has mastered the basic technique you can start doing work in hand without the side-reins, by placing the outside rein over the neck about two hands' breadth behind the poll. This is ideal if the horse has been worked under saddle beforehand.

Work in hand without side-reins: the outside rein is put across the neck about two hands' widths behind the poll.

• Instead of a lunge-rein or the reins, you can also work a horse in hand on a lead-rein.

The triangular (or Phillips) rein.

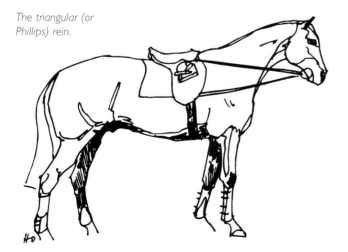

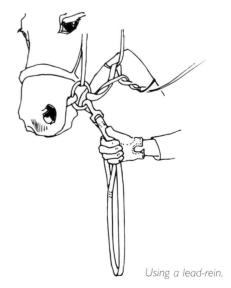

Using a lead-rein.

• *We recommend wearing gloves for work in hand.* Metal parts and buckles can easily injure your hands, and not only would this be uncomfortable and painful, it might also impair your ability to handle the horse skilfully.

• A part of the correct basic technique is the position of the trainer: *the right position is to stand by the horse's head with your shoulder towards the horse.*

• In this position you should walk quietly backwards, alongside the horse's movement, keeping a sympathetic and calm contact with the horse's mouth – it is not you who should be performing the piaffe, it is the horse who should do it!

Take care: Always look at the whole horse, not only the hind legs – observe especially his face, his posture, the way he carries his tail and how he breathes.

• Activate the horse with your voice (for example by clicking), and with the special whip for work in hand.

• *As regards vocal aids* it is very important that, just as in lungeing, you *always use the same words*, and, most of all, the same tone of voice: for the move-off, for instance, use a short 'Walk on!' with the voice staying high; for the halt, a long 'Haaalt!' in a lower tone.

• In praising the horse with your voice you should also always use the same word, for instance 'Goood!', and lower your voice.

• *Basically it doesn't matter what you say; what is important is how you say it, and the tone of voice.*

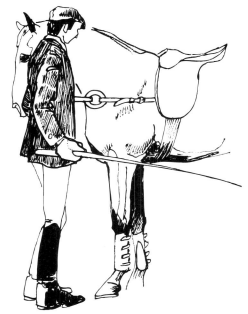

The correct position for work in hand.

• Always try to make do with a minimum of aids; at first ask your horse with just your voice, and only then use the whip, if it is really necessary.

• *Touch him with the whip at different spots and find out which ones he responds to best*: below or above the hock, on the thigh or just behind the

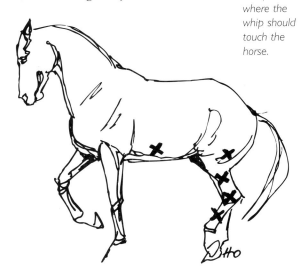

The places where the whip should touch the horse.

The horse should step from one diagonal to the other with great presence.

girth. At times it can be useful to use different points, for example across the quarters on the outside if the horse is falling out to the outside.

• The horse must respect the whip, but on no account should he become frightened of it.

• Always use the whip at the moment each hind leg leaves the ground.

• Do not give whip aids with the same intensity all the time, but vary them according to the desired effect and the horse's sensitivity and response. Here, too, remember the principle of training your horse to respond to increasingly subtle aids.

• In co-ordination with the driving aids you should catch the forward movement with a supple hand (no tension in your wrist, elbow and shoulder joints!), backwards and upwards in the direction of the poll.

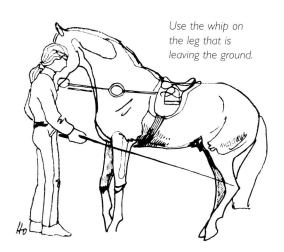

Use the whip on the leg that is leaving the ground.

Remember: Never drive more impulsion into your hand than you can handle easily.

• Praise the horse for the smallest progress – and on no account practise for more than five minutes at a time.

• In the first stages of this work it is recommended that you alternate regularly between in-hand work and lungeing the horse in a forward pace; in which case you should use a lunge-rein for the work in hand. To have a better feel for the horse's mouth, hold the lunge-line between thumb and forefinger, with the loops between the forefinger and middle finger – that is, with the remaining three fingers.

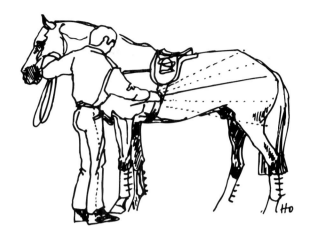

• Then let the horse step round you repeatedly, first in walk, later in trot.

• The following method has proved to be good: *before going onto the track start to develop initial collection by making the horse move laterally round you on a volte in trot.* You do this by leading the forehand gradually towards the outside so that the horse is performing shoulder-in on a volte.

• In this way practise moving off, and

Running the work-in-hand whip over the horse's quarters.

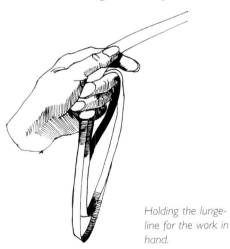

Holding the lunge-line for the work in hand.

• As a rule start on the left rein, but work the horse equally on both reins right from the beginning.

• The *correct method* is to begin by getting the horse used to the work-in-hand whip. Run the whip repeatedly over the horse's quarters and hind legs, until he ceases to show any signs of alarm.

Moving the horse laterally around you on a volte.

Shortened steps as a progression from shoulder-in.

step out of the volte onto the track so he takes a few shortened steps on the straight. Then on the track practise repeatedly the transition from halt into collected trot. As always, you should start this exercise on the left rein.

• From this point, gradually develop the shortened, collected steps on the track into a forward piaffe.

• If any problems occur – for example, if the horse starts to pull backwards, or runs to the inside (against the whip), or refuses to go forwards – you should come back to a volte and the exercise where the horse moves laterally round you (close to shoulder-fore on a volte), in order to bring the horse back into a rhythmical forward pace.

• When the horse has learned the piaffe going forwards in hand, then he can be mounted by a lightweight rider, who for the moment should only sit passively and sympathetically while you continue to work the horse in hand.

• Make your aids from the ground increasingly light, and gradually allow the horse to work more independently

then bringing the horse back to a halt again with a gentle hand; repeat this exercise several times. After a short while you will find that the horse will 'push himself off the hand' more and more lightly and become increasingly responsive to the aids.

• Once the shoulder-in is established you should lead the forehand increasingly in front of the hind legs and in time the horse will come to take several very collected, shortened, but energetic steps; after which you should immediately stop and praise the horse.

• Gradually you should let the horse

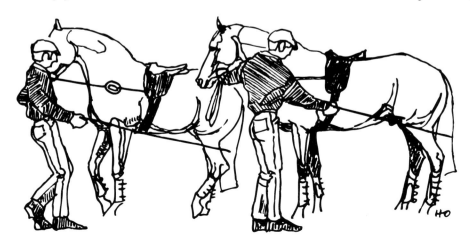

Shortened, very collected steps from halt on the track.

Work in hand under a lightweight rider.

under the rider who must sit lightly and sympathetically. At the same time the horse can learn to get used to the aids of the rider.

Remember: The horse must never be allowed to come to rely on the supporting aids from the ground to the extent that he will not respond to the rider's aids alone. The aim of the work in hand is that he will in the end perform the exercise solely in response to the rider's aids.

• In the further training of piaffe and passage under the rider it can be useful to have an experienced and skilful helper to support and control the work from the ground.

Remember: After the collecting work in hand the horse must also be encouraged to relax at the end of the session – that is, be allowed to stretch whether he is on the lunge or under saddle. The final ten minutes of walk are, of course, as essential as in the work under the rider!

PROBLEMS AND TIPS

PROBLEM

The horse tries to run away.

TIPS

• Check if fear is the cause.

• Reduce your demands; for instance when you repeat a movement don't ask

With the rider's weight on his back the horse will lose presence and lightness at first.

him to sustain it for so long.

• Drive the horse on less, and only use your voice.

• Leave the track and go back to the shoulder-in exercise on the volte.

• Check the side-reins and lengthen them, if necessary.

• Use the whip with less force and/or touch the horse in different places (experiment and find out which are the ones he responds to best).

PROBLEM

The horse goes backwards.

TIPS

• Position yourself behind the horse's eye.

• Re-establish forward movement by repeating shoulder-in on the volte exercise.

• If necessary lengthen the side-reins – the horse's nose should always be in front of the vertical.

• Give more frequent, but lighter half-halts.

PROBLEM

• The horse falls out to the outside, towards the wall.

TIPS

• Shorten the outside side-rein by up to five holes. This also helps if the horse is falling onto his outside shoulder.

• Touch the horse with the whip on the outside of the quarters across the back.

PROBLEM

The horse leans towards the inside.

TIPS

• Again, use the shoulder-in on the volte exercise to teach the horse to go away from the whip.

• If it is the forehand that is falling in, you should press against the horse's inside cheek and lead him back towards the outside.

PROBLEM

The horse's steps are not equal.

TIPS

• Check that the horse is straight: if the steps are not equal, this means that one of his hind legs is carrying more weight.

• Make sure that the track is level.

• Make the side-reins the same length: side-reins that are even make control easier.

• Make sure that you change the rein regularly.

PROBLEM

The horse is rushing.

TIPS

• Allow him to become calmer. Drive him on less and do not worry about the expressiveness for a while.

• Do not 'click' faster than you want the rhythm to be.

5.2 LATERAL MOVEMENTS

5.2.1 SHOULDER-IN

Precondition: Before you start riding shoulder-in, the horse must have learnt to carry more weight with the inside hind foot both on a circle and in a volte.

• To *prepare* for shoulder-in you should practise shoulder-fore, in which the horse is only slightly flexed and bent (less than in the shoulder-in). The inside hind foot steps towards the middle of the front legs.

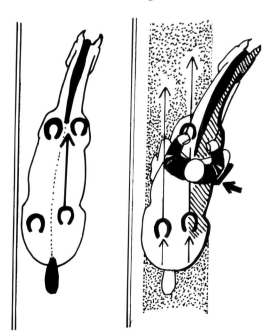

Correct shoulder-fore (left) and shoulder-in (right).

• Shoulder-fore, and decreasing and increasing the circle, can already be ridden as part of the horse's elementary training, to prepare him for other movements, and as a straightening exercise.

Procedure: When you begin shoulder-in, you should first show the horse or the young rider the exercise in walk.

• *In trot, shoulder-in is best practised on the circle*. Going through shoulder-fore you gradually ask for more angle (up to one step), while rhythm and bend must be preserved. This you should practise frequently but not for too long, making sure that you alternate each time between the lateral movement and riding forwards on a straight line.

• As soon as the horse can carry himself effortlessly in shoulder-in on the circle, you can start practising the exercise on the long side of the arena.

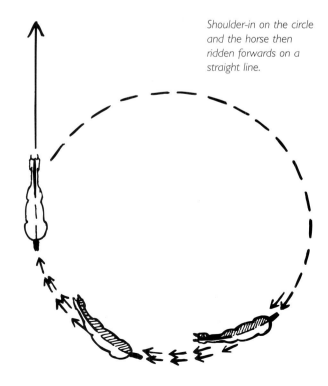

Shoulder-in on the circle and the horse then ridden forwards on a straight line.

Shoulder-fore is the movement used first in all work to make the horse perfectly straight.

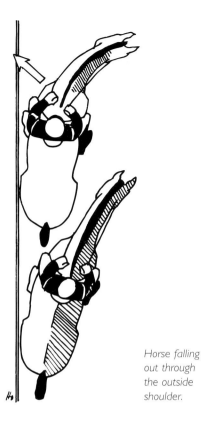

Horse falling out through the outside shoulder.

• **To perfect the exercise**, take care that the horse, while remaining evenly bent, moves so that his hind legs stay on one line in the middle of the track.

• With inexperienced riders you should practise the start of shoulder-in and then a subsequent straightening, so that they learn to lead the forehand towards the inside, not to push the quarters out.

• To finish shoulder-in, the outside rein and inside leg lead the forehand back onto the track.

PROBLEMS AND TIPS

PROBLEM

The horse's outside shoulder is falling out.

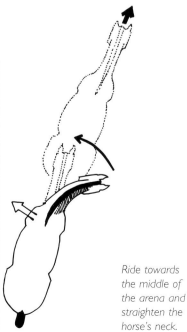

Ride towards the middle of the arena and straighten the horse's neck.

TIPS

• By opening and closing the outside hand in the contact you can control the neck on the outside.

• Finish the shoulder-in by straightening the neck and riding to the inside of the arena. Then start a new shoulder-in.

PROBLEM

The horse's hind legs step towards the outside – that is, they are not staying in the middle of the track.

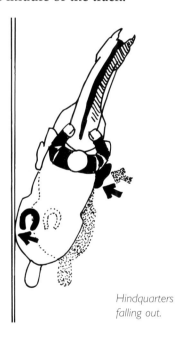

Hindquarters falling out.

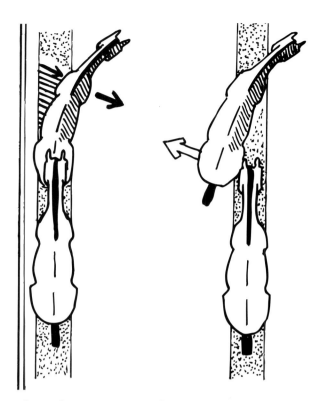

Start by leading the forehand towards the inside (left), not by pushing the hindquarters out (right).

TIPS

In starting the shoulder-in, lead the forehand to the inside; do not push the hindquarters to the outside.

• Take care that you do not take your inside leg back, but keep it in the line shoulder-hip-heel.

• Check the position and the supporting function of your outside leg.

PROBLEM

The horse is wobbling in shoulder-in; he does not stay steadily on one line.

TIPS

• Do shoulder-in for shorter stretches to ensure that the horse is able to balance himself.

• Fix your eyes on a point, and then follow the line to this point. This can also help when you are doing shoulder-in away from any boundary, for example down the centre line.

PROBLEM

You are losing the bend.

Shoulder-in is sometimes called the 'mother' of all lateral movements.

TIPS

• Turn onto a volte, and then take the bend from that into shoulder-in.

• Go back onto a circle and develop shoulder-in anew out of shoulder-fore.

• Start the exercise just after a corner, and take the bend from the corner into shoulder-in.

PROBLEM

The movement is lacking fluency.

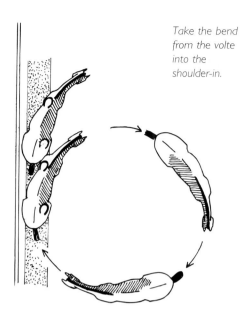

Take the bend from the volte into the shoulder-in.

Maintain the bend as you come out of the corner.

TIPS

• Ask for just a short stretch of shoulder-in at a time, and then regain impulsion in a forward pace.

• Begin the movement in a somewhat stronger tempo.

5.2.2 TRAVERS AND RENVERS

Travers is the preliminary stage to half-pass.

Precondition: the horse can start to learn travers if he can do shoulder-in at least for short stretches.

• In his elementary training your horse should already have learnt to move away from your outside leg promptly in such exercises as the half-pirouette in walk, and decreasing the circle.

• To begin with, both horse and young

rider should be taught travers in walk. Walk is also a good gait in which to refine the aids later on.

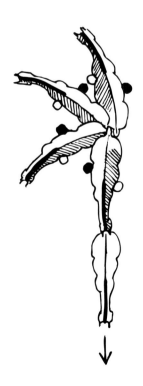

Half-pirouette in walk.

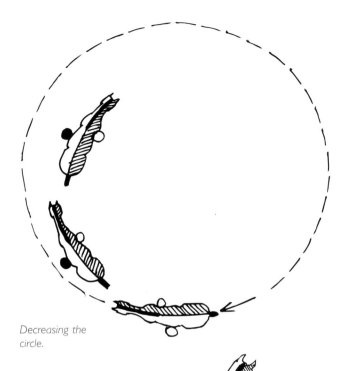

Decreasing the circle.

• *Like shoulder-in, start by asking for travers little and often, and on the circle*; thus you can use the lateral bend which is already established. It is important that the influence of your outside leg is consistent and subtle.

• First ask with your inside leg for shoulder-fore then use your outside leg to make the horse's outside hind foot step in towards the middle of the front legs. Do not ask for too great an angle to begin with.

Remember: Your inside leg creates lateral bend and forward movement.

• To help the rider to activate his inside leg, it is advisable to increase the circle while riding travers.

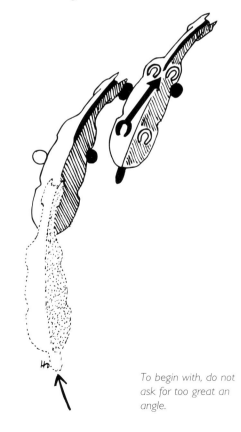

Start by asking for travers little and often, and on a circle.

To begin with, do not ask for too great an angle.

Travers is the exercise that prepares the horse for the half-pass.

• To begin with, ride travers for just a short while each time, alternating with movements to develop impulsion (Schwung). Used like this travers is a good gymnastic exercise.

• Once travers on the circle is successful, take it onto a straight line for a few strides. If your horse loses his flexion and bend, you will have to go back to preparing the exercise on the circle.

Renvers is travers to the other side. For example, the horse is on the left rein, but bent and flexed to the right instead of the left – that is, in the direction of travel. Instead of the front legs, the hind legs stay on the track.

In travers it is the hindquarters which are led onto the second track, whereas in renvers it is the forehand. To complete renvers, align the forehand with the hindquarters (the first principle in straightening the horse).

• Renvers is a good exercise for providing variety in the practice of lateral movements; in using it you will advance the fine co-ordination of your aids, and your horse's submissiveness (Durchlässigkeit) and ability to concentrate.

• It is different from travers in that in the practising phase the horse is less likely to confuse the aids with those for the strike-off into canter. However, the gymnastic value, the aids and the degree of difficulty are no different to travers, and so this exercise will not be mentioned separately any more.

• Before you lead the forehand from the track towards the inside of the arena, you should flex your horse to

Renvers.

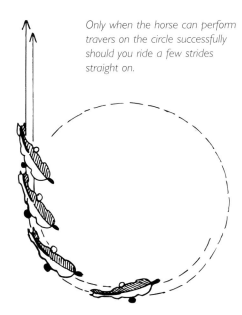

Only when the horse can perform travers on the circle successfully should you ride a few strides straight on.

the outside and 'feel through' with what will be your inside leg. Using shoulder-fore towards the wall, you can prepare the bend smoothly.

Remember: This exercise is – like travers – more demanding than shoulder-in and should therefore only be ridden for a short while each time, and in alternation with exercises that develop impulsion (Schwung).

PROBLEMS AND TIPS

PROBLEM

In the transition to travers the horse starts to canter.

TIPS

• Check your leg aids. Make sure you are just holding your legs in easy rhythm with the trot, and not pressing, otherwise your horse can confuse the aids for travers with those for canter.

In renvers the forehand is led towards the inside of the arena to begin with.

• For a while ride more renvers than travers.

PROBLEM

The horse is losing flexion and bend.

TIPS

• Finish the exercise, and then try once more to influence and hold the horse with the inside leg in shoulder-fore.

• If you have just started travers, go back to preparing it on the circle. It is more valuable to practise the transition several times, than to ask the horse to perform it for long stretches.

• Hold and maintain the flexion and

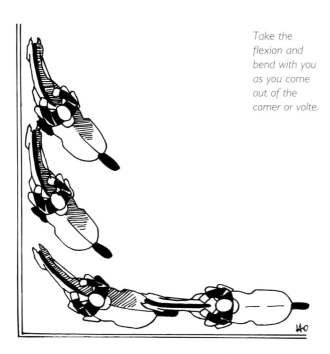

Take the flexion and bend with you as you come out of the corner or volte.

bend as you come out of a corner or volte.

• Have great patience with short-coupled horses, which have more problems with this exercise.

PROBLEM

The horse loses fluency.

TIPS

• Ride the movement for a shorter stretch at a time.

• Generate more impulsion (Schwung) at the beginning of travers.

• Some horses shorten too much in this exercise; with these it is a good idea to practise it in rising trot at first.

• Check the flexion! The outside hind foot should step towards the inside front foot: therefore from the front you should see three, and not four, legs.

5.2.3 HALF-PASS

Half-pass is demanded in collected trot, and later in collected canter.

Precondition: You can start to practise half-pass once your horse can do shoulder-in and travers.

There are several different exercises involving half-pass:

– *the short half-pass*: from the centre line to the track, or vice versa;

– *the double short half-pass*: a short half-pass from the centre line to the track and another one back to the centre line (or vice versa);

– *the long half-pass*: across a whole diagonal, for example M to K;

– *the zig-zag half-pass*: to the right and left of the centre line; it is measured in trot in metres and in canter in strides (jumps);

– *the double long half-pass*: for example K to B and then to H; this is only demanded in the more difficult tests.

Aids: Everybody thinks of the outside leg but at least as important is the inside leg, because this causes the lateral bend and the forward movement (fluency).

Feel your inside knee slightly lower, so that your weight stays on the inside – your horse will want to step towards your centre of gravity.

Let the outside rein allow the neck to stretch for the flexion and bend, and use the inside rein with care. If the bend is established, the horse will maintain the flexion by himself.

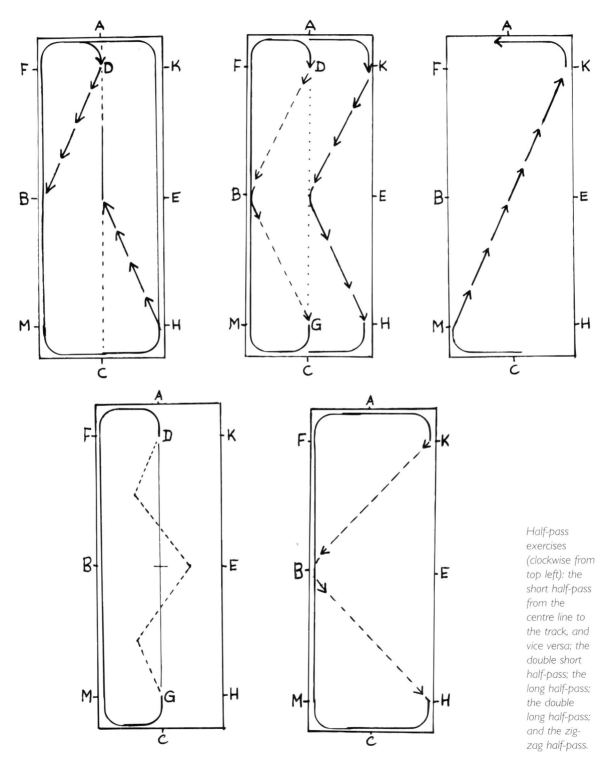

Half-pass exercises (clockwise from top left): the short half-pass from the centre line to the track, and vice versa; the double short half-pass; the long half-pass; the double long half-pass; and the zig-zag half-pass.

• Because your horse will find it easier to perform half-pass in trot, you should only start with canter half-pass when the half-pass in trot is well established.

• *A good exercise to develop the half-pass is to ride it out of a travers on the circle*: ride several lengths of half-pass out of travers towards the open side of the circle and into the arena. You can start and finish at any given point, as long as the rhythm, fluency and a constant flexion and bend are maintained.

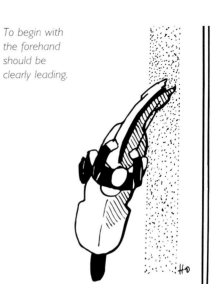

To begin with the forehand should be clearly leading.

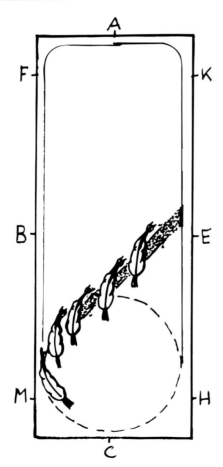

Transition from travers on the circle to half-pass.

When rhythm, fluency or lateral bend are lost, you should stop and prepare a new transition.

• In the initial stage you should ride the half-pass well forwards and less sideways. The forehand should be clearly leading at first.

Excellent lateral bend, fluency and collection in half-pass. (Dr Reiner Klimke on Pascal.)

Remember: To begin with, a few lengths of half-pass are sufficient.

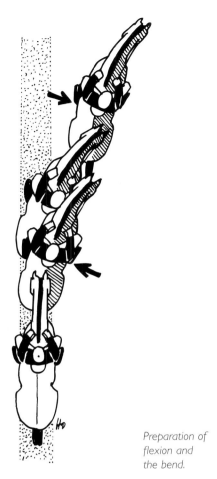

Preparation of flexion and the bend.

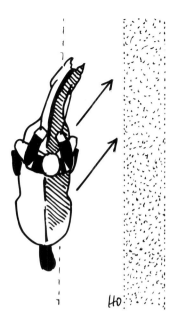

In its most polished form the half-pass is ridden parallel to the track.

• The short half-pass should be started from the centre line towards the track.

• Before that, shorten the inside rein, apply the inside leg to put the horse in shoulder-fore (not shoulder-in!) and so prepare the flexion and lateral bend.

• Only when the horse is maintaining rhythm, bend and fluency in response to increasingly subtle aids in half-pass, should you eventually ride a prescribed course exactly to a marker.

• Whilst to start with, the forehand should be a good stride ahead, eventually the half-pass should be ridden increasingly parallel to the track.

• Only when the horse can perform the short half-passes successfully in both directions should the double short half-pass be attempted.

• In the change of direction in double short half-pass and zig-zag half-pass, you can prevent the horse from leading with his hindquarters in the following way: first flex the horse in the new direction, and only then change your legs for the new lateral bend and sideways movement. In short: first hands – then legs!

• *For the half-pass in canter you will achieve a far more immediate response if you influence the horse with both legs.* Always start with the outside leg, and drive him in the canter rhythm into the inside leg; thus your inside leg always influences the hind foot that is leaving the ground.

• For the zig-zag half-pass in canter you should straighten your horse in the last canter stride before the change of direction, and only after that ride the flying change. In the half-pass with four strides on each side of the centre line, for instance, you should be counting '1,2,3, straight!' and then let the next stride come out in the new direction.

PROBLEMS AND TIPS

PROBLEM

The horse is losing his rhythm – that is, the steps are becoming unlevel or he is starting to rush.

TIPS

• Reduce your demands, and once more establish the shoulder-in and travers. If need be, ask for less angle in travers at first, so that the horse's ligaments, tendons and joints can become used to the unusual strain gradually.

• Again, let the forehand lead for a good stride, before asking for a more parallel movement.

PROBLEM

The hindquarters are leading in the transition.

TIPS

• Train your own awareness by having your transitions checked repeatedly from the ground, or by looking back yourself.

• Start the half-pass out of shoulder-fore – that is, always apply the inside leg before using the outside one for the sideways movement.

• If this should happen because your horse is anticipating the exercise, change the place where you practise it, or sometimes stay in shoulder-fore.

PROBLEM

The horse is not moving sideways sufficiently, so there is not enough room to complete the exercise.

TIPS

• First, teach your horse to respond to more subtle sideways-driving aids in walk.

• Plan your tactics: for example, in the double short half-pass it is better to start immediately after the corner, rather than to be short of room in the second short half-pass and lose rhythm and fluency.

• The same applies to the zig-zag half-pass: start the first half-pass immediately on reaching the centre line instead of at D, for example.

PROBLEM

Your horse is tilting his head and becoming crooked, for instance the right ear is lower.

TIPS

• Improve lateral suppleness by working on curved lines (for example circles and voltes), and practising shoulder-fore and shoulder-in.

• To correct the fault momentarily, take your right hand slightly higher; moreover this has more impact if you hold the rein so it passes over the top of

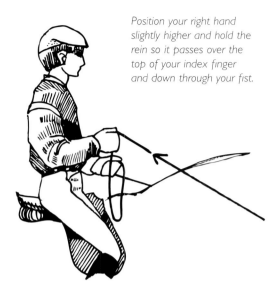

Position your right hand slightly higher and hold the rein so it passes over the top of your index finger and down through your fist.

your index finger and down through your fist.

• Straighten the horse temporarily, continue the half-pass without flexion, then renew the proper flexion.

PROBLEM

The horse loses lateral bend.

TIPS

• In your preparatory work practise travers more frequently.

• Remember to use your inside leg rhythmically and elastically.

• As soon as the horse loses lateral bend, ride a circle and then take the bend into the half-pass.

• Changing repeatedly between shoulder-fore and half-pass also has a good gymnastic effect.

• For competitions you can – temporarily! – hide the fault slightly by flexing your horse's neck more.

PROBLEM

The half-pass lacks fluency.

TIPS

• Start the half-pass in a slightly stronger pace.

• Even in the training of an older horse you should regularly ride the half-pass for a longer stretch in a forward pace, for instance from the centre line to the last marker of the long side, to improve fluency.

PROBLEM

In the zig-zag half-pass your horse anticipates and throws himself into the new direction.

TIPS

• Interrupt the half-pass and ride a few lengths of shoulder-fore.

• In canter, take care that your horse does not change by himself. Vary the number of strides on each side of the centre line.

5.3   FLYING CHANGES

5.3.1 SINGLE FLYING CHANGES

Consider the following observations:

• *Often the training of flying changes is left much too late.* The flying change is something a horse performs quite naturally, and young horses running

All the criteria for a good flying change are fulfilled: rhythm, looseness (Losgelassenheit), straightness and balance in an 'uphill' canter.

Opposite: The right moment to give the aids for the flying change is when the horse has three legs on the ground. (Nicole Uphoff-Becker on Rembrandt – both pictures.)

free in a field can be observed doing flying changes without the influence of a rider on their back.

• Many riders make the mistake of schooling exclusively for counter canter, especially for dressage tests. They systematically stop their horses from changing in the way that young horses change naturally while running in the field. They might even have punished them for it, yet now the horses are suddenly asked to perform the forbidden movement – which will inevitably lead to misunderstandings and problems.

• *The best time to start flying changes is when you are beginning to practise counter canter and your horse still has the natural tendency to change into true canter.* This means you are

teaching the flying change at the same time as you are beginning to teach counter canter – the condition being, of course, that you yourself know how to ride flying changes. If this is not the case, you should seek help from an experienced trainer.

• When your horse has understood the flying change on both reins, proceed very calmly to establish the counter canter, which to be performed correctly does nevertheless require an established collected canter.

• For single flying changes the degree of collection does not need to be high. A young horse with a good canter, and which is balanced and performs the transition into canter in response to subtle aids, can easily learn flying changes in working canter.

• The feared un-asked-for changing in counter canter ceases by itself with increasing submissiveness (Durchlässigkeit), collection and growing obedience, but it is recommended that you stop practising newly introduced flying changes about fourteen days before entering an elementary test.

> **IMPORTANT** Before any attempt is made to demand a flying change the horse's way of going must fulfil the following criteria:

1. The canter jump must be round, in three-beat, with a clearly discernible moment of suspension – that is, not too short.
2. Before every new attempt the horse must be completely relaxed and supple (losgelassen).
3. He must be completely straight – that is, he should jump with his hind legs towards his centre of gravity.
4. He must be balanced, which can be checked by giving and retaking the reins.

Summary

– Rhythm
– Relaxation, looseness (Losgelassenheit) and suppleness
– Straightness
– Balance

If the horse fails to comply with even just one of these points, then you should not ask for a flying change.

Aids
• There are several different ways of giving the aids for the flying change, and which you use depends on the method that was used when teaching the horse to do the movement. Most professional trainers teach the following aids: that the essential influence for the change comes from what will become your outside leg, which should be positioned a hand's breadth further back and pressing in the rhythm of the canter; your new inside leg just supports elastically on the girth. You should sit so that your weight follows the new canter stride in easy, supple rhythm.

Remember: Above all, avoid blocking the new lead by shifting your weight or changing the flexion too harshly.

• *Concentrate* on your newly positioned outside leg; the new inside one will fall into place by itself as long as you are sitting smoothly with the new canter. For a flying change to be successful, the *timing* of the aids is crucial: the horse can only change the canter lead in the moment of suspension, and inevitably he needs a moment to respond to your aids. Thus the closer to the moment of suspension you give the aids, the less time he has to organise himself: running away or changing late behind quite often result.

• *The right moment to apply the aid to change* – when you take your inside leg back so it becomes the new outside leg and apply pressure – *is the moment of support, when the horse has three legs on the ground*. This is exactly the moment in which your inside leg is driving the horse on in true canter. Just call the moment back into your consciousness, because you have already been giving the pressure with

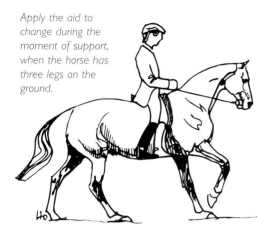

Apply the aid to change during the moment of support, when the horse has three legs on the ground.

the inside leg automatically at the right moment.

• For practice, the following *preliminary exercise* has proved valuable: the trainer makes the rider aware of how he is driving the horse forwards with the inside leg in true canter, and so tries to indicate to him exactly when it must be brought back in position to become the new outside leg. The best way to identify this is for the trainer to call out each time the right moment occurs – for example, call out 'Now'. As soon as the rider can feel the right moment, the trainer should encourage him to say 'Now' himself; then the trainer can ask him to take his leg back at the same time.

• The aids are best checked on a circle. It is useful if the rider counts in time with the rhythm and then simulates on 'four' the aids for a flying change. Thus at the same time he is prepared for counting the sequence changes later on.

Methods of training
• *Prepare the horse by asking for frequent transitions into canter on both reins, all the while making the horse*

sensitive to barely noticeable aids, and starting with your outside leg. Build up to simple changes of leg in canter.

• Always ride the first flying changes towards the horse's better side. Most horses are crooked to the right, so you should change from the right into the left canter. If this change works, stop and praise the horse. Then try the change from the left rein to the right – not in the same session to begin with, but rather the next day.

• To start with, always practise the flying change in the same place; only when the horse has understood the exercise should you change in different places. You should also ride the same figure several times without a change at all in order to prevent the horse running off or anticipating the change.

• In the first attempts it is of the utmost importance that the horse does not change late behind. Other problems – if he should become faster, or does not stay completely straight – can be corrected and improved upon later.

> **IMPORTANT**   After the first successful attempt you should stop immediately and praise the horse.

• If the horse changes late behind, the flying change should be prepared again – calmly and without punishing him. The flying change is an exercise which demands a quick response and fast reflexes on the horse's part (in contrast to exercises of strength such as piaffe); if you punish the horse, his response would contain a measure of fear which would inhibit the change or prevent it altogether.

To begin with, the most important thing is that the horse does not change late behind.

a shallow loop on the long side, to ask for the change about one length after leaving the track, and to ride a transition to walk as soon as the flying change succeeds.

• If communication difficulties arise, the following exercise can be of help: start a change of rein out of the corner and ride back to the track close to travers; on reaching the track give the aids for a flying change. As soon as the horse has understood the aids you should practise on a straight line.

• When schooling, always ride flying changes at the end of the session so that you can stop and praise the horse after the first successful attempt. In these circumstances this pause benefits the horse's learning process, and is more important for this reason than as an interval of rest necessitated by his gymnastic exertions.

The following method has proved to be the best in the training of flying changes: ride a transition from walk to counter canter at the beginning of the long side, canter on for a few lengths, then turn onto a half circle (20m diameter) and let the horse change the canter towards the wall (on reaching the track).

• With well-balanced young horses, which have a good canter jump, it will almost always lead to success if in a playful way you change the rein on a short diagonal in working canter and attempt the flying change just before reaching the track.

• Another well-tried method is to start

A reliable training method: in counter canter turn onto a half circle and let the horse change on reaching the track.

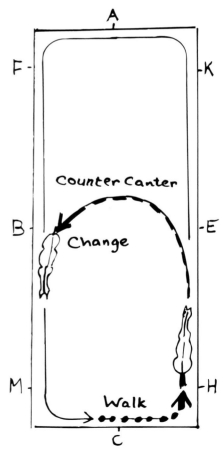

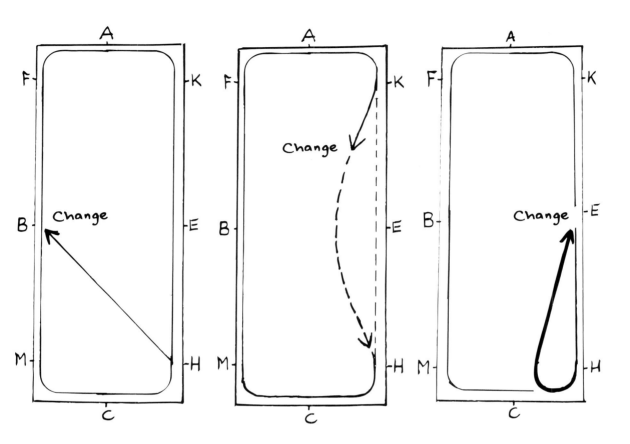

• *It is not recommended* that you practise flying changes with a pronounced change of direction (such as changing the rein from circle to circle or through the circle), because horses tend to change with the inside front leg, while changing late behind.

• Should your horse start to anticipate a change after a few attempts and become excited, try riding less conventional diagonals (see page 136) as this sort of freestyle can have a positive effect: for example, after the second corner of the short side, ride to the middle of the opposite short side, or go from the point between H and B to C or A, or vice versa. Stay on the same rein until the horse is completely calm:

only then should you ride a flying change and thus change the rein. Besides, riding these lines provides you with an excellent opportunity to straighten the horse before the flying change, by riding him close to shoulder-fore.

• *In time the aids should become increasingly subtle and invisible*, and the changes performed in different places. Take care that your horse is executing the changes precisely, straight, at a constant pace, calmly, well forward and uphill. This refinement can only be achieved through careful straightening work.

Check your technique!

Left: Change of rein from H to B – change just before the track.

Centre: Ride a shallow loop and ask for the change about one length after leaving the track.

Right: Turn out of the corner and ride back to the track in slight travers and change on reaching the track.

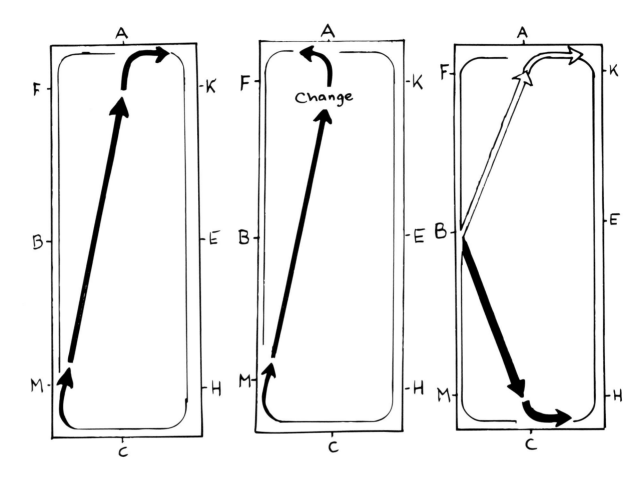

Above left: 'Freestyle' diagonal ridden without a change of rein.

Centre: Change of rein with a flying change.

Right: A good opportunity for straightening the horse by riding slightly shoulder-fore.

Remember: If your horse has not yet mastered the flying change on both reins reliably, you must check if he is changing late behind.

• If the new inside hind foot is coming forward only a tiny moment later than the equivalent front leg, the rider cannot feel it. As changing late behind must on no account be allowed to creep in, you should therefore ask somebody to watch you, who can recognise clearly how the flying change is being jumped.

• You can also check what is happening in a mirror in an indoor arena. For instance, you can change

from counter canter on the circle in the middle of the arena to true canter on reaching the track in front of the mirror.

PROBLEMS AND TIPS

In principle: When problems arise, check carefully that the horse's way of going meets the criteria mentioned on p.132. Try different methods if one does not lead to success. An instructor of less experienced riders should always remember to check the timing of the aids.

PROBLEM

Your horse is changing late behind.

TIPS

• Make him change on the track from true canter to counter canter towards the wall. It is important to check this.

• If a horse is not used to this method, and is not changing but instead becoming faster, you should first re-establish a completely steady canter

Checking the flying change in front of the mirror.

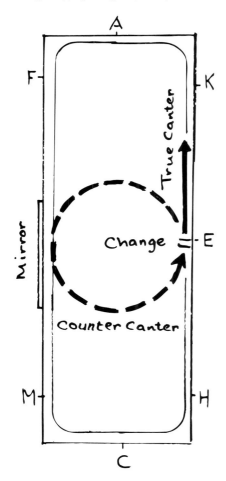

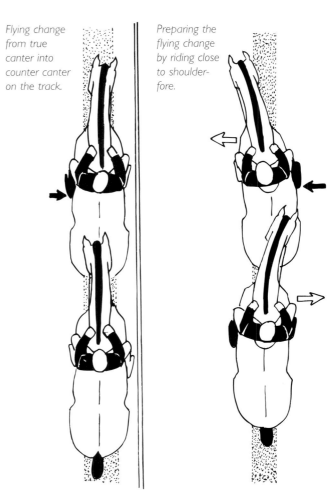

Flying change from true canter into counter canter on the track.

Preparing the flying change by riding close to shoulder-fore.

rhythm, concentrate on correctly co-ordinated aids, and then make another attempt.

• You can support the aids on what has become the horse's outside rein, with the whip.

PROBLEM

Your horse does not remain straight when jumping the change.

TIPS

• Prepare the change by riding close to

shoulder-fore, and support the new canter stride with your inside leg, again towards shoulder-fore.

• In a change towards the outside of the arena, use the wall.

• Increase the basic tempo slightly.

PROBLEM

Your horse is becoming faster in the flying change; he is running away.

TIPS

• If it is a young horse which has just started to learn flying changes, this is no reason for concern as he will get better with increasing experience.

• With an older horse which is already used to flying changes, you should ride the diagonal described earlier, from the beginning of the long side to the middle of the short side of the arena, without a change of rein, until your horse ceases to get excited. Only then should you change the rein and the canter lead.

• Do not practise flying changes too often in the same place.

PROBLEM

Your horse is delaying the flying change (taking one or two canter strides after you have given the aids).

TIP

• Go back to making the horse as sensitive as possible to the aids for strike-off into canter, for example with frequent simple changes. Especially in view of sequence changes which come

next in training, you must insist on your horse performing the flying change in immediate response to your aids.

PROBLEM

Your horse is jumping the change with too high a croup.

TIP

• You should lengthen the strides slightly for the change. This can also help if the change is being jumped in too flat a manner.

5.3.2 FLYING CHANGE SEQUENCES

Precondition: Only when the horse can perform single changes faultlessly and at any given point should sequence changes be practised.

Flying change sequences should only be attempted when the horse's way of going fulfils the four criteria already discussed. That is:

– Rhythm
_ Relaxation, looseness (Losgelassenheit) and suppleness
– Straightness
– Balance

• In proceeding from single to multiple changes you should ride them predominantly going large and on the track.

• Only if the changes from the inside to the outside are insufficiently established, should you use the inner (5m) track to begin with.

• Initially you should ride changes at intervals of about half an arena or every ten canter strides.

• In the course of training these intervals may be progressively reduced until a change is asked at every fifth, then every fourth canter stride. How much you increase your demands should always be dictated by how many strides you need until the horse's way of going once again meets the criteria recalled above.

• To begin with, do not ride changes to the outside leg in the corners.

• After a number of four-time changes you should ride them away from the track, that is, on the diagonal.

• Only when the horse can perform really polished and accurate four-time changes should you attempt three-time and finally two-time changes.

• If problems arise, for instance if the horse becomes crooked, you should interrupt the sequence immediately, go back to the track, ride shoulder-fore and then some single changes in shoulder-fore.

• At the first sign of crookedness on the diagonal or the centre line, make sure that you look at a point straight in front of you and that you are riding forwards sufficiently.

Remember: In flying change sequences *do not shorten the canter too much* – do not make it unnecessarily difficult for your horse by shortening the moment of suspension!

• Your aids for the change must not be too strong and thus upset the horse in any way. Make it your aim to become progressively more subtle with your aids. This also applies to your outside leg, which you take backwards to an increasingly lesser degree.

• Never practise sequence changes for too long, and do remember to interchange the exercise with lengthening in true canter at regular intervals.

• After the first successful sequence of flying changes you should immediately stop the horse and praise him, for exactly the same reasons as when you were practising single changes.

• When your horse is jumping two-time changes without fault, you can start practising one-time (tempi) changes (flying changes from stride to stride).

• With horses which are crooked to the right, you should start on the left rein, that is to say, you let the horse jump the first change towards his better side. The best way is to ride a change to the right and then back to the left into true canter after the second corner of the short side, and do it always at the same spot. If you do not succeed straightaway, then you will have enough time on the rest of the long side to try again.

• Shortly before the exercise, use some sort of voice aid such as clicking to gain your horse's attention, because in this very fast sequence of movements he has to co-operate wholeheartedly.

• After a while, try this single one-time change on the other rein.

• When this works well on both reins,

you can start adding another one, and so on.

• When you can do about five or six one-time changes, you can progress to practising them on the diagonal and add yet more, until you can manage as many as might be required.

• In the one-time changes it has proved most effective to keep both legs in the backward position and to give the aids merely with pressure from your 'new' outside to your inside leg: in this way you can apply them more quickly, sit quietly and your horse stays straight.

• To facilitate the timing and *counting technique* for flying change sequences – for example, for five four-time changes – count in the following way: 1, 2, 3, 4 – 2, 2, 3, 4 – 3, 2, 3, 4 – 4, 2, 3, 4 – 5, 2, 3, 4. For timing the changes to fit on the diagonal proceed as follows: do two four-time changes before X, the third at X and the last couple after it.

• In counting three-time changes, proceed in the same say: 1, 2, 3 – 2, 2, 3 – 3, 2, 3 and so on. For five three-time changes on the diagonal the third occur at X, the first two before, and the last two after X.

• You should keep the two-time rhythm for the two-time changes in the back of your head like this: 1 hm, 2 hm, 3 hm and so on, although you can also count 1, 2 – 2, 2 – 3, 2 – 4, 2 and so on. And again, you should plan the changes on the diagonal in such a way that the middle one is jumped at X; thus with nine two-time changes, for instance it would be the fifth, and with fifteen one-time changes it would be eighth change which is at X.

PROBLEMS AND TIPS

In principle: Problems with flying change sequences should basically be approached in the same way as those encountered with single changes. Most of all be sure that your horse's way of going does fulfil the four essential criteria already discussed.

PROBLEM

Your horse has got into the habit of not responding absolutely spot-on

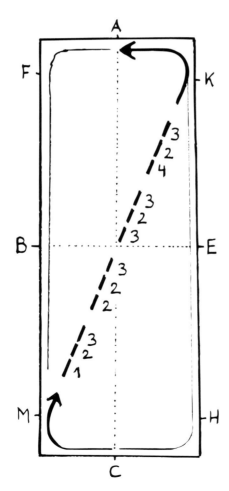

Fitting in three-time changes across the diagonal.

immediately to the aids, but of **changing about one canter stride after.**

TIPS

• You might be able to get away with this in the single changes at the lower levels, but for sequence changes you must categorically instil upon the horse that he responds promptly to your aids! To do this you had best go back onto the circle, where you can get after him more energetically.

• Once he responds to the aids as you want, you should repeat the change with more subtle aids.

PROBLEM

Your horse is holding back and then jumps the flying change with his quarters too high.

TIPS

• As with single changes, increase the basic tempo.

• Then ride the change with your legs and use your back to drive the horse on. You must first prepare the horse for this aid in true canter.

PROBLEM

In between the sequence changes your horse is jumping a canter stride too many or too few.

TIPS

• Canter on quietly, and as you would in a dressage test, try to continue the sequence correctly.

• Then very calmly commence a new sequence.

PROBLEM

Soon after your horse has learned to do one-time changes, he becomes confused with two-time changes and repeatedly jumps a one-time change in between.

TIP

• Do not worry about this too much! Especially with keen horses, this is quite normal and will cease after a time by itself. Nevertheless: do not practise one-time changes close to a competition where you are riding a test that only demands two-time changes.

5.4 CANTER PIROUETTES

The canter pirouette is purely an *exercise of strength* and therefore requires a relatively long gymnastic preparation.

• It relies upon the horse being able to maintain a collected and cadenced canter by himself, and to keep cantering at the same tempo whilst the rider's legs do no more than breathe with the rhythm. With the lightest and most discreet of aids you must be able to shift more and more weight onto his quarters. Make sure that you are not supporting him in any way with your hands, and that throughout the movement you have the feeling of being able to give and retake the reins (which does not mean you should actually do this all the time!).

• **Aids:** You should influence the horse with both your legs. Always start with the outside leg, and drive him in the canter rhythm towards your inside leg. Thus each leg rhythmically engages the horse's hind foot that is leaving the ground.

Support the horse well with the outside rein; the inside rein leads the forehand in the rhythm of the pace around the hind legs, and must get lighter with each canter jump. Keep your weight slightly more on your inside seat bone, so that the horse can jump towards your centre of gravity.

• The best *preparation* for the pirouette is the 'pirouette canter': canter straight and almost on the spot for a few strides (three to four for the half-pirouette, six to eight canter strides for the pirouette), before demanding the additional difficulty of rotation, the turn around the inside hind foot on the smallest possible circle.

Remember: As mentioned above, ***do not support the horse in any way with your hands*** (have that feeling of giving and retaking the reins)! Canter increasingly on the spot.

• Experiment as to how much or how little you can best use your weight in this canter. Thus on one occasion make a transition to walk, praise the horse and give him long rein, on the next ride him forwards directly and praise him. To begin with you should practise the 'pirouette canter' on the circle, later on a straight line as well.

• You should also ride this exercise in the horse's further training as a direct preparation for every canter pirouette, though always remember that it takes a

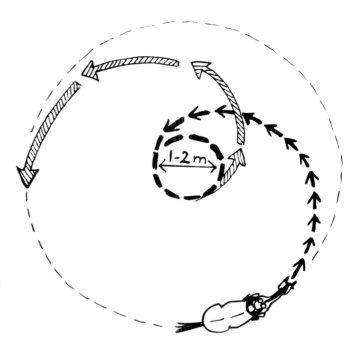

Decreasing the circle in preparation for the canter pirouette.

great deal of strength. One or two canter strides ridden almost on the spot are a sufficient preparation, before you lead the forehand sideways into the pirouette.

Summary: *Your horse must first be mature and strong enough to perform this movement:* only then can you attempt to lead the forehand sideways and let him jump into the turn around the inside hind foot.

• *Here is another good way to prepare the horse*: from a high degree of collection in canter, decrease the circle until its diameter is about 1-2m; although how small you can make it will always depend on the activity of the inside hind foot, the rhythm and the contact. Afterwards increase the circle by lengthening the stride, and then praise the horse.

• To begin with, you should not

Opposite: The canter pirouette should be ridden in a clear three-beat and with a high degree of collection. (Karin Rehbein on Donnerhall.)

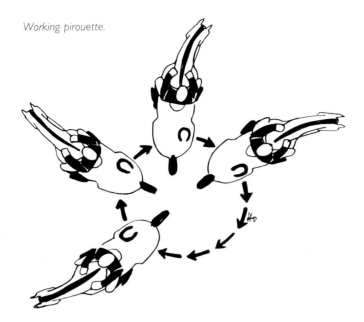

Working pirouette.

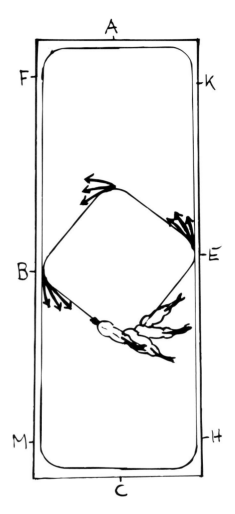

Circle ridden as a square: in the corners lead the forehand sideways for two or three strides.

practise this more than once or twice on each rein, and then ride forwards on a straight line.

• Even at a later stage of training you should always ride a (larger) *working pirouette* first, before you ask for pirouettes on a tighter circle.

• The *objectives* remain the same: distinctive, rhythmical jumps, bend through the haunches, and a light and elastic contact.

• *Another good preparatory exercise*, which in training you should ride quite frequently: ride a few strides of canter almost on the spot, then two or three strides leading the forehand sideways – make the number of strides depend on how long you can maintain rhythm and cadence. Afterwards ride on in a more forward pace. For this exercise you can also ride a circle as a square, leading the forehand sideways for two or three jumps in each the corner and then riding on straight again.

Take great care: Always finish by riding forwards, and, especially with an exercise of strength like the pirouette, consider the following: to begin with, never demand two exercises of strength consecutively – for instance do not ride piaffe or passage immediately after a canter pirouette. Alternate with other exercises that your horse already knows, or with those that need a quick reaction such as flying changes.

PROBLEMS AND TIPS

PROBLEM

The horse throws himself into the pirouette; he does not wait for your aids.

TIPS

• Remember to keep a good contact on the outside rein.

• Check the number of jumps asked for (half-pirouette, three to four canter strides; pirouette, six to eight canter strides).

• In training vary the number of jumps: ride sometimes more, sometimes fewer canter strides.

• As soon as your horse starts to hurry, use the outside rein to ride out of the turn at any point and then try again.

PROBLEM

The horse becomes excited, wants to run off in the pirouette and does not stay in one place.

TIP

• Make a transition to walk and then

For the pirouette the horse must have acheived the necessary collection while being able to maintain clear, rhythmical canter jumps and a soft contact (as shown here by Herbert Rehbein and Gassendi).

prepare a new canter pirouette. Practise on the bigger circle of the working pirouette.

PROBLEM

The inside hind foot is 'stuck'; it is not moving up and down with each stride.

TIPS

• Check that all the conditions and the preparation are right.

• Consider whether you have demanded too tight a pirouette too early. Go back to the working pirouette.

• Decrease the circle down to a working pirouette around a helper, who can, if required, support your aids with a work-in-hand whip from the ground.

PROBLEM

Your horse is jumping too many strides on the spot, without coming into the turn.

TIPS

• Check your weight aids.

• Take care to lead the horse clearly into the turn with the inside rein, which you then release.

5.5 THE PIAFFE

When to start teaching piaffe under a rider depends on the conformation, temperament and general training of the horse. As a rule, though, the horse should not be younger than six years old, and he should be able to do any exercises of Medium level. The preparatory work in hand can be started as soon as the basic training is complete.

• Attempting ridden piaffe presupposes that the degree of straightness, collection and sensitivity to the aids has progressed far enough for the horse to move off in trot rhythm from halt and walk in response to merely indicative aids, and to be able to offer half steps in the downward transition from trot.

• These half steps are by no means only useful with respect to the piaffe, but are in general an excellent gymnastic exercise to aid submissiveness (Durchlässigkeit) and the carrying capacity of the hindquarters.

• *Criteria* for the piaffe are above all rhythm, and the bend through the haunches (hip and stifle joint). *How high the horse steps depends on his conformation and the manner in which he moves himself.* Ideally the hind foot is lifted to the height of the middle of the other hind fetlock, and the diagonal front leg to the middle of the other front cannon bone.

Remember: Envisage a horse walking uphill: the raising of the forehand is a consequence of the increased bend through the haunches and is relative to it – that is why it is called relative elevation. By raising the forehand excessively you are blocking the hind legs and putting pressure on the horse's back.

• Give the *aids* for piaffe from a quiet and sympathetic seat – that is, without

*Klaus
Balkenhohl on
Goldstern in
piaffe.*

disturbing the horse and thus making it more difficult for him to balance.

• Most of all do not sit too heavily to begin with, but allow the horse's back to swing.

• *Allow both your legs to stay in elastic, even rhythm with the horse, and keep them in their normal position.* This position is important in relation to passage, because for passage you take your legs back slightly further so that your horse can clearly understand the difference between the aids for piaffe and those for passage.

Take care: Some horses find it easier if the rider applies his leg aids diagonally. The best way to find out is to try it!

• *Do not allow the horse to become at all heavy in your hands*, but maintain an absolutely constant and light contact. Even in this, the highest degree of collection the horse should always be ready to go forwards and to stretch downwards – the forward tendency must be maintained and you should be able to lengthen the topline of the horse's neck by about a hand's breadth.

A helper on the ground can touch each hind foot with the whip as it leaves the ground.

• *Your voice aids should also be carefully considered*: clicking, for instance, reserve mainly for half steps and piaffe; an encouraging 'Go on', too, can help your horse to maintain these half steps or a piaffe. After all, you are trying to manage with increasingly subtle aids, and your horse has to learn to co-operate with you more and more.

• *The whip should be used sparingly* and only applied – whether by the rider or from the ground – to the hind foot about to leave the ground. It also makes sense to have someone on the ground to support and check your aids.

Good piaffe.

Incorrect piaffe.

Rhythm is an essential criterion for the piaffe.

• There are different *methods* for practising the piaffe: the one which entails least strain on the horse is the work in hand without a rider. Later during the work in hand you can put

The horse must always be ready to go forward and stretch if asked.

up a rider who will sit in a sympathetic and passive way and then slowly and progressively you can let the aids from the ground be replaced by the rider's influence.

• *For the ridden piaffe the same principles apply as for the work in hand*: practise frequently but never for too long, and let your first priority be to stop and praise the horse at the smallest improvement, especially to begin with. The horse must be given every chance to understand what is being asked of him, and you must let him know at once when he has done well.

• The *best preliminary exercise for the piaffe* is contained in the half steps, which can be developed from collected

'Piaff', ridden by Lieselott Linsenhoff (now Rheinberger), does honour to his name: a piaffe as it is very rarely seen.

trot, from walk or halt.

• You can decrease the length of the collected trot steps with half-halts. With this method you run the least risk of failure!

Remember: If you are asking for half steps from walk, you must first shorten the walk.

• You can also develop these short, very collected steps from halt. With subtle aids ask your horse to move off repeatedly in trot rhythm, then to come back to halt; hold him back a little, if his temperament requires it, and shorten his steps progressively.

• Before you practise these half steps and the subsequent piaffe from halt, your horse must be completely

submissive (durchlässig) and on the bit. Only use this method in moderation, otherwise you might easily provoke resistance.

• What you must do is to find out which method suits your horse the best.

• It is very much recommended to *ring the changes between the various methods*, so that the horse does not learn to anticipate your intentions. In particular this can happen when you practise the movement frequently from walk or halt, and can lead to problems such as fidgeting in walk whenever you shorten the reins, or restlessness in the halt.

• *When finishing a series of half steps you should also introduce variety:* after

To begin with, rhythm is more important than presence/ expression.

a few good steps, sometimes ride a downward transition to halt or walk, praise the horse and give him a long rein; at others, ride forwards into a quiet trot rhythm and so regain impulsion (Schwung).

• Do not start to think of the piaffe too early on when practising these half steps – the piaffe must develop very gradually out of these half steps.

• Over a period of time, ask for the half steps increasingly on the spot, until a few steps of forward piaffe result.

• A very good exercise to ride as preparation for the piaffe: *repeatedly shorten the pace by giving subtle half-halts, then increase it again after a few lengths*. In this way you also avoid a

high croup and stiffness in the haunches.

Take care: never practise the piaffe for too long at any one time! Even in tests no more than fifteen steps are demanded. Avoid overtaxing the horse with this exercise of strength. ***Even in advanced training, five minutes are enough***.

• Variety is almost as important as not going on for too long. Never forget that this exercise of the highest collection should always be followed by a period of riding forwards and regaining impulsion (Schwung).

• Also remember to vary the exercises: after a few successful steps of piaffe, go back to exercises with which the horse is already familiar. And to begin with, above all *take care not to demand another exercise of strength such as the canter pirouette in the same session*, because you would overtax the carrying capacity of the hindquarters.

• At first you will always practise the piaffe with a clear forward tendency over a stretch of one or two metres. It requires long, patient training until a horse can perform the piaffe correctly on the spot.

• *Take special care to maintain a quiet and constant rhythm in the piaffe*. The principle of rhythm being given priority over expression/presence is most important and applies equally to both piaffe and passage.

• As a trainer you should also realise that *many horses will never perform a really expressive piaffe on account of their conformation and the way they move*. With a rhythmically correct piaffe they can still, however, achieve marks of 5 or 6.

• The work to refine the piaffe and enhance its expressiveness can begin when seven or eight steps over a stretch of about a metre can be successfully achieved – reliably, in rhythm, with a forward tendency and in response to fairly light aids.

• Then you should try to increase the number of steps up to fifteen, and to ride them more and more on the spot.

• Finally you should increasingly work to incorporate piaffe into the context of a dressage test, and to perform it precisely at predetermined points in the arena.

PROBLEMS AND TIPS

In principle: If problems with piaffe arise, the reason is usually that you have been proceeding too fast. *That is why you should go back one training stage as soon as problems occur*. Most of all practise establishing collection by shortening the steps but with rhythm and energy, and out of that the impulsion for balanced forward movement.

Remember: Even in the piaffe on the spot your horse must always be ready to move forwards again. Help your practice with accompanying work in hand.

• The worst result of incompetent and overhasty procedure is when the forelegs cross over each other, which – once established – can rarely be corrected. If you keep that in mind, you will certainly find it easier to accept that you must train the piaffe with care.

PROBLEM

Your horse is becoming unlevel.

TIPS

• Check the straightness – if your horse is taking irregular steps, one hind leg is carrying more weight than the other.

• Change the whip to the other side from time to time, so that you are not always activating only one hind leg.

• Check your contact: it must be completely constant and even, so that your horse is absolutely straight.

Crookedness: one hind leg is carrying more weight than the other.

PROBLEM

Your horse is hurrying the steps or tip-toeing.

TIPS

• You have been proceeding too fast and should go back to preliminary exercises, then increase your demands gradually.

• Take care not to drive the horse on, or to click faster than in trot. Remember: the rhythm is quite likely to be rather slower than in trot.

• Each time your horse trips, ride forwards calmly out of the piaffe. Go back to the shortened steps. As soon as irregularities in the rhythm occur, ride rhythmically forwards again.

PROBLEM

Your horse's hind legs 'stick' to the ground – mainly in connection with stiff haunches and a high croup.

TIPS

• Let your horse go forwards more. Go back one training stage.

• Maybe you were riding him with too strong a rein contact.

• Check the degree of elevation. If necessary, lengthen the topline of the neck by a hand's breadth.

PROBLEM

Your horse is resisting, even tries to rear.

TIPS

• Create a deeper and rounder outline before riding piaffe.

• Ride more forwards.

PROBLEM

Your horse is evading sideways or stepping backwards.

TIPS

• Go back to developing half steps from collected trot, then ride on out of it in a clear rhythm.

• Check the contact (which should be constant and light) and the horse's straightness.

PROBLEM

The horse's legs are not lifted up as diagonal pairs.

TIP

• Go back to work in hand for a while.

Ride the piaffe with a clear forward tendency.

PROBLEM

Your horse knows the test and is offering the piaffe before the required point.

TIPS

• In training, do not always ride the same sequence of exercises.

• Ride on from that point and practise the piaffe at a later point.

5.6 PASSAGE

From experience we can assert that to perform the passage, the horse as a rule must be able to perform the piaffe, at least in forward movement (1-2m). The fact that the passage can be practised much less in hand, that is, without the weight of a rider, would also support this order in training.

An excited horse offering passage steps.

• Nevertheless, a combination of the rider's aids and work in hand (with an assistant on the ground) has proved very successful.

• *If during an earlier stage in training, particularly whilst working on piaffe, your horse gets excited and offers a passage, quietly make the most of it and go along with it*; and then remember to praise the horse and to ride forwards into a rhythmical trot, or to ride a downward transition to walk. This means you are accepting it momentarily, but then go back to working systematically on the piaffe, and enjoy your horse's promising talent for the passage.

• **Criteria** for the passage are above all, rhythmical diagonal steps, the bend through the haunches (hip and stifle joint), and the cadence that results from the long moment of suspension created each time the horse springs from one diagonal pair of legs to the other.

• *In the passage, even more so than in piaffe, how high the horse steps depends on his conformation and the way in which he moves.* Some horses do passage with a very high action of the front legs, while others tend to stretch them forwards more. Ideally the hind hoof should come up to the middle of the opposite fetlock, and the diagonal front leg should be lifted so that the forearm is horizontal.

• You should be giving your **aids** just as you would in the piaffe, from a supple, sympathetic seat.

Above all, you must not sit too heavily, but rather should make yourself light in the saddle and almost think of rising trot. In this way you encourage the prolonged moment of suspension to be sustained as long as possible, as if you were taking your horse upwards with you.

• In order to support the rhythm of the passage you may – especially in the practice phase – move both your hands upwards slightly with the rhythm of the movement.

Remember: You must never apply pressure with your back and legs, but should allow the passage rhythm with sympathetic, quiet and supple aids, and initially support the rhythm with your voice.

• It has proved useful to touch the horse with a whip on the highest point of the croup, either from the saddle or from the ground. Even this, however, does not work with every horse. You simply have to find out yourself!

• *Experiment, too,* as to whether the horse reacts better to diagonal or equilateral leg aids.

• For the passage you should take your legs further back, so that the horse can easily tell the difference between the aids for piaffe and those for passage.

• The *training procedure* is in principle the same as for piaffe: *after the first few successful steps you should stop and praise your horse;* increase your demands on his efforts only very gradually, and let your first priority be to keep your horse happy and willing in his work.

• There are several different possibilities regarding ways to develop the passage.

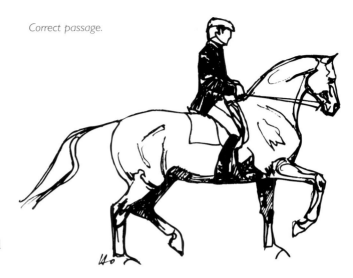

Correct passage.

• You can gradually allow the steps out forwards from the piaffe.

• From collected trot, bring the steps into the passage rhythm by gradually increasing the collection even more. Before that, however, the horse must be well prepared through frequent riding of transitions and variations within a

In the passage, rhythm takes precedence over expression in the early stages.

A good passage, full of expression.

A well-executed passage. (Erika Taylor and Crown Law.)

(Schwung) is taken into the passage steps, so they become increasingly cadenced and expressive.

• Some trainers develop the passage from collected walk. This certainly cannot be a generally recommended method, however, as the horse does not have much impulsion (Schwung) in walk.

• Just as when you are working to perfect the piaffe, the number of steps should be increased only gradually.

Passage with good expression.

pace, and thereby made completely submissive (durchlässig) and always ready to collect.

• With some horses it is more successful to shorten them up straightaway after lengthened strides in trot. In this way the impulsion

To perform to exact markers, and to execute all the figures and correct transitions with the precision demanded at Grand Prix level, the horse has to have the time to mature.

PROBLEMS AND TIPS

In principle: Most problems arise for the same reasons as they do in piaffe. And for passage, too, the same principle applies: *whenever problems* *occur, go back a stage in training, and ride more forward again.* Forgo any attempt at higher expressiveness if it can only be achieved at the cost of the rhythm. Here, too, some horses are limited in what they can do because of their conformation and the way they move.

PROBLEM

Your horse is going with irregular steps.

TIPS

• Check the straightness, so that one hind leg does not have to carry more weight than the other.

• Because of the increased moment of suspension your horse will be particularly sensitive to an uneven contact.

• As in the piaffe, change the whip to your other side from time to time.

Allow the topline of the neck to become a hand's width longer.

PROBLEM

Your horse is going with stiff, dragging hind legs.

TIP

• Check the head and neck carriage, which in this exercise can easily be too high. If necessary, allow the topline of the neck to become a hand's breadth longer.

INDEX

Page numbers in *italic* indicate illustrations